ON THE FUTURE OF OUR EDUCATIONAL INSTITUTIONS; HOMER AND CLASSICAL PHILOLOGY

First published 1909
This edition published by Lector House in 2024

ISBN: 978-93-6138-195-9

Lector House LLP
Registered Office: H. No. 96, Block C, Tomar Colony,
Burari, Delhi – 110084, India
info@lectorhouse.com
www.lectorhouse.com

ON THE FUTURE OF OUR EDUCATIONAL INSTITUTIONS; HOMER AND CLASSICAL PHILOLOGY

FRIEDRICH WILHELM NIETZSCHE,
JOHN MCFARLAND KENNEDY,
OSCAR LEVY

2024

LECTOR HOUSE LLP

ON THE FUTURE OF OUR EDUCATIONAL INSTITUTIONS

HOMER AND CLASSICAL PHILOLOGY

BY

FRIEDRICH NIETZSCHE

TRANSLATED, WITH INTRODUCTION, BY
J. M. KENNEDY

EDITED BY
DR OSCAR LEVY

Translator's Introduction.

"On the Future of our Educational Institutions" comprehends a series of five lectures delivered by Nietzsche when Professor of Classical Philology at Băle University. As they were prepared when he was only twenty-seven years of age, we can scarcely expect to find in them that broad, "good European" point of view which we meet with in his later works. These lectures, however, are not only highly interesting in themselves; but indispensable for those who wish to trace the gradual development of Nietzsche's thought.

Nietzsche's aim, as is now pretty well known, was the elevation of the type man. At this period of his life he believed that this end could be best attained by the protection and careful development of men of genius, Hence his antagonism in the following lectures towards the purely time-serving German schools and colleges of his age, in which culture was not only neglected but not even known—the one aim of the teachers being to instruct the pupils in the art of "getting on," of playing a successful part in the struggle for existence, of becoming useful citizens. Of course, Nietzsche was too little of a wild reformer to be adverse to a schooling of this nature. He freely admits that a bread-winning education is necessary for the majority, and that officials are necessary to the State; but he adds that everything learnt as a preparation for taking part in the commercial or political battle of life has nothing to do with culture. True culture is only for a few select minds, which it is necessary to bring together under the protecting roof of an institution that shall prcparc thcm for culturc, and for culture only. Such an institution, he goes on to say, does not yet exist; but we must have it if the delicate flower of the German mind is no longer to be choked by the noxious weeds which have gathered round it. As instances of minds thus "choked," Nietzsche mentions Lessing, Winckelmann, and Schiller.

The standard of culture to be aimed at by the man of genius Nietzsche had in mind was to be found in the model literary and artistic works which have come down to us from ancient Greece. To understand these works, of course, the classical authors had to be studied in the original, and the methods of teaching then in vogue paid too much attention to inconsequential points (*e.g.* variant readings) instead of dealing with the subject in a broad-minded philosophical spirit. Nietzsche endeavoured to counteract this tendency in the "Homer and Classical Philology," his inaugural address at Bâle University, by outlining a much vaster conception of philology than his fellow-teachers had ever dreamt of, laying stress upon the *artistic* results which would accrue if the science were applied on a wider scale—results which would be of a much higher order than those obtained by the narrow pedantry then prevailing.

It is a very superficial comment on these lectures to say that Nietzsche was merely referring to the German schools and colleges of his time. It would be even shallower to suggest that his remarks do not apply to the schools and teachers of present-day England and America; for we likewise do not possess the cultural institution, the *real* educational establishment, that Nietzsche longed for. Broadly speaking, the English public schools, the older English universities, and the American high schools, train their scholars to be useful to the State: the modern universities and the remaining schools give that instructionin bread-winning which Nietzsche admits to be necessary for the majority; but in no case is an attempt made to pick out a few higher minds and train them for culture. Our crude methods of teaching the classical languages are too well known to be commented upon; and an insight into classical antiquity, with the good taste, the firm principles, and the lofty aims obtained therefrom, is exactly what our various educational institutions do not aim at giving. Yet, as Nietzsche truly says, no progress in any other direction, no matter how brilliant, can deliver our students from the curse of an education which adapts itself more and more to the needs of the age, and thus loses all its power of guiding the age. Let the student who, as the victim of this system, suffers more from it than his teachers care to admit, read the paragraph on pp. 79 and 80 containing the sentences—

> He feels that he can neither lead nor help himself.... His condition is undignified, even dreadful: he keeps between the two extremes of work at high pressure and a state of melancholy enervation.... He seeks consolation in hasty and

incessant action so as to hide himself from himself, etc.,

and then let him confess that Nietzsche's insight into his psychology is profound and decisive. The whole paragraph might have been written by Nietzsche after a visit to present-day England.

As bearing upon the same subject, the reader will find it interesting to compare the lectures here translated with Matthew Arnold's prose writings passim, particularly the *Essays in Criticism, Mixed Essays,* and *Culture and Anarchy*.

J. M. KENNEDY.

LONDON, May 1909.

Contents

ON THE FUTURE OF OUR EDUCATIONAL INSTITUTIONS

Preface.

(To be read before the lectures, although it in no way relates to them.)

THE reader from whom I expect something must possess three qualities: he must be calm and must read without haste; he must not be ever interposing his own personality and his own special "culture"; and he must not expect as the ultimate results of his study of these pages that he will be presented with a set of new formulæ. I do not propose to furnish formulæ or new plans of study for *Gymnasia* or other schools; and I am much more inclined to admire the extraordinary power of those who are able to cover the whole distance between the depths of empiricism and the heights of special culture-problems, and who again descend to the level of the driest rules and the most neatly expressed formulæ. I shall be content if only I can ascend a tolerably lofty mountain, from the summit of which, after having recovered my breath, I may obtain a general survey of the ground; for I shall never be able, in this book, to satisfy the votaries of tabulated rules. Indeed, I see a time coming when serious men, working together in the service of a completely rejuvenated and purified culture, may again become the directors of a system of everyday instruction, calculated to promote that culture; and they will probably be compelled once more to draw up sets of rules: but how remote this time now seems! And what may not happen meanwhile! It is just possible that between now and then all *Gymnasia*—yea, and perhaps all universities, may be destroyed, or have become so utterly transformed that their very regulations may, in the eyes of future generations, seem to be but the relics of the cave-dwellers' age.

This book is intended for calm readers,—for men who have not yet been drawn into the mad headlong rush of our hurry-skurrying age, and who do not experience any idolatrous delight in throwing themselves beneath its chariot-wheels. It is for men, therefore, who are not accustomed to estimate the value of everything according to the amount of time it either saves or wastes. In short, it is for the few. These, we believe, "still have time." Without any qualms of conscience they may improve the most fruitful and vigorous hours of their day in meditating on the future of our education; they may even believe when the evening has come that they have used their day in the most dignified and useful way, namely, in the *meditatio generis futuri*. No one among them has yet forgotten to think while reading a book; he still understands the secret of reading between the lines, and is indeed so generous in what he himself brings to his study, that he continues to reflect upon what he has read, perhaps long after he has laid the book aside. And he does this, not because he wishes to write a criticism about it or even another book; but simply because reflection is a pleasant pastime to him. Frivolous spendthrift! Thou art a reader after my own heart; for thou wilt be patient enough to accompany an author any distance, even though he himself cannot yet see the goal at which he is aiming,—even though he himself feels only that he must at all events honestly believe in a goal, in order that a future and possibly very remote generation may come face to face with that towards which we are now blindly and instinctively groping. Should any reader demur and suggest that all that is required is prompt and bold reform; should he imagine that a new "organisation" introduced by the State, were all that is necessary, then we fear he would have misunderstood not only the author but the very nature of the problem under consideration.

The third and most important stipulation is, that he should in no case be constantly bringing himself and his own "culture" forward, after the style of most modern men, as the correct standard and measure of all things. We would have him so highly educated that he could even think meanly of his education or despise it altogether. Only thus would he be able to trust entirely to the author's guidance; for it is only by virtue of ignorance and his consciousness of ignorance, that the latter can dare to make himself heard. Finally, the author would wish his reader to be fully alive to the specific character of our present barbarism and of that which distinguishes us, as the barbarians of the nineteenth century, from other barbarians.

Now, with this book in his hand, the writer seeks all those who may happen to be wandering, hither and thither, impelled by feelings similar to his own. Allow yourselves to be discovered—ye lonely ones in whose existence I believe! Ye unselfish ones, suffering in yourselves from the corruption of the German spirit! Ye contemplative ones who cannot, with hasty glances, turn your eyes swiftly from one surface to another! Ye lofty thinkers, of whom Aristotle said that ye wander through life vacillating and inactive so long as no great honour or glorious Cause calleth you to deeds! It is you I summon! Refrain this once from seeking refuge in your lairs of solitude and dark misgivings. Bethink you that this book was framed to be your herald. When ye shall go forth to battle in your full panoply, who among you will not rejoice in looking back upon the herald who rallied you?

Introduction.

THE title I gave to these lectures ought, like all titles, to have been as definite, as plain, and as significant as possible; now, however, I observe that owing to a certain excess of precision, in its present form it is too short and consequently misleading. My first duty therefore will be to explain the title, together with the object of these lectures, to you, and to apologise for being obliged to do this. When I promised to speak to you concerning the future of our educational institutions, I was not thinking especially of the evolution of our particular institutions in Bâle. However frequently my general observations may seem to bear particular application to our own conditions here, I personally have no desire to draw these inferences, and do not wish to be held responsible if they should be drawn, for the simple reason that I consider myself still far too much an inexperienced stranger among you, and much too superficially acquainted with your methods, to pretend to pass judgment upon any such special order of scholastic establishments, or to predict the probable course their development will follow. On the other hand, I know full well under what distinguished auspices I have to deliver these lectures—namely, in a city which is striving to educate and enlighten its inhabitants on a scale so magnificently out of proportion to its size, that it must put all larger cities to shame. This being so, I presume I am justified in assuming that in a quarter where so much is *done* for the things of which I wish to speak, people must also *think* a good deal about them. My desire—yea, my very first condition, therefore, would be to become united in spirit with those who have not only thought very deeply upon educational problems, but have also the will to promote what they think to be right by all the means in their power. And, in view of the difficulties of my task and the limited time at my disposal, to such listeners, alone, in my audience, shall I be able to make myself understood—and even then, it will be on condition that they shall guess what I can do no more than suggest, that they shall supply what I am compelled to omit; in brief, that they shall need but to be reminded and not to be taught. Thus, while I disclaim all desire of being taken for an uninvited adviser on questions relating to the schools and the University of Bâle, I repudiate even more emphatically still the rôle of a prophet standing on the horizon of civilisation and pretending to predict the future of education and of scholastic organisation. I can no more project my vision through such vast periods of time than I can rely upon its accuracy when it is brought too close to an object under examination. With my title: *Our* Educational Institutions, I wish to refer neither to the establishments in Bâle nor to the incalculably vast number of other scholastic institutions which exist throughout the nations of the world to-day; but I wish to refer to *German institutions* of the kind which we rejoice in here. It is their future that will now engage our attention, *i.e.* the future of German elementary, secondary, and public schools (Gymnasien) and universities. While pursuing our discussion, however, we shall for once avoid all comparisons and valuations, and guard more especially against that flattering illusion that our conditions should be regarded as the standard for all others and as surpassing them. Let it suffice that they are our institutions, that they have not become a part of ourselves by mere accident, and were not laid upon us like a garment; but that they are living monuments of important steps in the progress of civilisation, in some respects even the furniture of a bygone age, and as such link us with the past of our people, and are such a sacred and venerable legacy that I can only undertake to speak of the future of our educational institutions in the sense of their being a most probable approximation to the ideal spirit which gave them birth. I am, moreover, convinced that the numerous alterations which have been introduced into these institutions within recent years, with the view of bringing them up-to-date, are for the most part but distortions and aberrations of the originally sublime tendencies given to them at their foundation. And what we dare to hope from the future, in this behalf, partakes so much of the nature of a rejuvenation, a reviviscence, and a refining of the spirit of Germany that, as a result of this very process, our educational institutions may also be indirectly remoulded and born again, so as to appear at once old and new, whereas now they only profess to be "modern" or "up-to-date."

Now it is only in the spirit of the hope above mentioned that I wish to speak of the future of our educational institutions: and this is the second point in regard to which I must tender an apology from the outset. The "prophet" pose is such a presumptuous one that it seems almost ridiculous to deny that

I have the intention of adopting it. No one should attempt to describe the future of our education, and the means and methods of instruction relating thereto, in a prophetic spirit, unless he can prove that the picture he draws already exists in germ to-day, and that all that is required is the extension and development of this embryo if the necessary modifications are to be produced in schools and other educational institutions. All I ask, is, like a Roman haruspex, to be allowed to steal glimpses of the future out of the very entrails of existing conditions, which, in this case, means no more than to hand the laurels of victory to any one of the many forces tending to make itself felt in our present educational system, despite the fact that the force in question may be neither a favourite, an esteemed, nor a very extensive one. I confidently assert that it will be victorious, however, because it has the strongest and mightiest of all allies in nature herself; and in this respect it were well did we not forget that scores of the very first principles of our modern educational methods are thoroughly artificial, and that the most fatal weaknesses of the present day are to be ascribed to this artificiality. He who feels in complete harmony with the present state of affairs and who acquiesces in it *as something* "*selbstverständliches*,"[1] excites our envy neither in regard to his faith nor in regard to that egregious word "*selbstverständlich*," so frequently heard in fashionable circles.

He, however, who holds the opposite view and is therefore in despair, does not need to fight any longer: all he requires is to give himself up to solitude in order soon to be alone. Albeit, between those who take everything for granted and these anchorites, there stand the *fighters*—that is to say, those who still have hope, and as the noblest and sublimest example of this class, we recognise Schiller as he is described by Goethe in his "Epilogue to the Bell."

"Brighter now glow'd his cheek, and still more bright
With that unchanging, ever youthful glow:—
That courage which o'ercomes, in hard-fought fight,
Sooner or later ev'ry earthly foe,—
That faith which soaring to the realms of light,
Now boldly presseth on, now bendeth low,
So that the good may work, wax, thrive amain,
So that the day the noble may attain."[2]

[1] Selbstverständlich = "granted or self-understood."

[2] *The Poems of Goethe.* Edgar Alfred Bowring's Translation. (Ed. 1853.)

I should like you to regard all I have just said as a kind of preface, the object of which is to illustrate the title of my lectures and to guard me against any possible misunderstanding and unjustified criticisms. And now, in order to give you a rough outline of the range of ideas from which I shall attempt to form a judgment concerning our educational institutions, before proceeding to disclose my views and turning from the title to the main theme, I shall lay a scheme before you which, like a coat of arms, will serve to warn all strangers who come to my door, as to the nature of the house they are about to enter, in case they may feel inclined, after having examined the device, to turn their backs on the premises that bear it. My scheme is as follows:—

Two seemingly antagonistic forces, equally deleterious in their actions and ultimately combining to produce their results, are at present ruling over our educational institutions, although these were based originally upon very different principles. These forces are: a striving to achieve the greatest possible *extension of education* on the one hand, and a tendency *to minimise and to weaken it* on the other. The first-named would fain spread learning among the greatest possible number of people, the second would compel education to renounce its highest and most independent claims in order to subordinate itself to the service of the State. In the face of these two antagonistic tendencies, we could but give ourselves up to despair, did we not see the possibility of promoting the cause of two other contending factors which are fortunately as completely German as they are rich in promises for the future; I refer to the present movement towards *limiting and concentrating* education as the antithesis of the first of the forces above mentioned, and that other movement towards the *strengthening and the independence* of education as the antithesis of the second force. If we should seek a warrant for our belief in the ultimate victory of the two last-named movements, we could find it in the fact that both of the forces which we hold to be deleterious are so opposed to the eternal purpose of nature as the concentration of education for the few is in harmony with it, and is true, whereas the first two forces could succeed only in founding a culture false to the root.

First Lecture.

(Delivered on the 16th of January 1872.)

Ladies and Gentlemen,—The subject I now propose to consider with you is such a serious and important one, and is in a sense so disquieting, that, like you, I would gladly turn to any one who could proffer some information concerning it,—were he ever so young, were his ideas ever so improbable—provided that he were able, by the exercise of his own faculties, to furnish some satisfactory and sufficient explanation. It is just possible that he may have had the opportunity of *hearing* sound views expressed in reference to the vexed question of the future of our educational institutions, and that he may wish to repeat them to you; he may even have had distinguished teachers, fully qualified to foretell what is to come, and, like the *haruspices* of Rome, able to do so after an inspection of the entrails of the Present.

Indeed, you yourselves may expect something of this kind from me. I happened once, in strange but perfectly harmless circumstances, to overhear a conversation on this subject between two remarkable men, and the more striking points of the discussion, together with their manner of handling the theme, are so indelibly imprinted on my memory that, whenever I reflect on these matters, I invariably find myself falling into their grooves of thought. I cannot, however, profess to have the same courageous confidence which they displayed, both in their daring utterance of forbidden truths, and in the still more daring conception of the hopes with which they astonished me. It therefore seemed to me to be in the highest degree important that a record of this conversation should be made, so that others might be incited to form a judgment concerning the striking views and conclusions it contains: and, to this end, I had special grounds for believing that I should do well to avail myself of the opportunity afforded by this course of lectures.

I am well aware of the nature of the community to whose serious consideration I now wish to commend that conversation—I know it to be a community which is striving to educate and enlighten its members on a scale so magnificently out of proportion to its size that it must put all larger cities to shame. This being so, I presume I may take it for granted that in a quarter where so much is *done* for the things of which I wish to speak, people must also *think* a good deal about them. In my account of the conversation already mentioned, I shall be able to make myself completely understood only to those among my audience who will be able to guess what I can do no more than suggest, who will supply what I am compelled to omit, and who, above all, need but to be reminded and not taught.

Listen, therefore, ladies and gentlemen, while I recount my harmless experience and the less harmless conversation between the two gentlemen whom, so far, I have not named.

Let us now imagine ourselves in the position of a young student—that is to say, in a position which, in our present age of bewildering movement and feverish excitability, has become an almost impossible one. It is necessary to have lived through it in order to believe that such careless self-lulling and comfortable indifference to the moment, or to time in general, are possible. In this condition I, and a friend about my own age, spent a year at the University of Bonn on the Rhine,—it was a year which, in its complete lack of plans and projects for the future, seems almost like a dream to me now—a dream framed, as it were, by two periods of growth. We two remained quiet and peaceful, although we were surrounded by fellows who in the main were very differently disposed, and from time to time we experienced considerable difficulty in meeting and resisting the somewhat too pressing advances of the young men of our own age. Now, however, that I can look upon the stand we had to take against these opposing forces, I cannot help associating them in my mind with those checks we are wont to receive in our dreams, as, for instance, when we imagine we are able to fly and yet feel ourselves held back by some incomprehensible power.

I and my friend had many reminiscences in common, and these dated from the period of our boyhood upwards. One of these I must relate to you, since it forms a sort of prelude to the harmless experience already mentioned. On the occasion of a certain journey up the Rhine, which we had made together one summer, it happened that he and I independently conceived the very same plan at the same hour and on the same spot, and we were so struck by this unwonted coincidence that we determined to carry the plan out forthwith. We resolved to found a kind of small club which would consist of ourselves and a few friends, and the object of which would be to provide us with a stable and binding organisation directing and adding interest to our creative impulses in art and literature; or, to put it more plainly: each of us would be pledged to present an original piece of work to the club once a month,—either a poem, a treatise, an architectural design, or a musical composition, upon which each of the others, in a friendly spirit, would have to pass free and unrestrained criticism.

We thus hoped, by means of mutual correction, to be able both to stimulate and to chasten our creative impulses and, as a matter of fact, the success of the scheme was such that we have both always felt a sort of respectful attachment for the hour and the place at which it first took shape in our minds.

This attachment was very soon transformed into a rite; for we all agreed to go, whenever it was possible to do so, once a year to that lonely spot near Rolandseck, where on that summer's day, while sitting together, lost in meditation, we were suddenly inspired by the same thought. Frankly speaking, the rules which were drawn up on the formation of the club were never very strictly observed; but owing to the very fact that we had many sins of omission on our conscience during our student-year in Bonn, when we were once more on the banks of the Rhine, we firmly resolved not only to observe our rule, but also to gratify our feelings and our sense of gratitude by reverently visiting that spot near Rolandseck on the day appointed.

It was, however, with some difficulty that we were able to carry our plans into execution; for, on the very day we had selected for our excursion, the large and lively students' association, which always hindered us in our flights, did their utmost to put obstacles in our way and to hold us back. Our association had organised a general holiday excursion to Rolandseck on the very day my friend and I had fixed upon, the object of the outing being to assemble all its members for the last time at the close of the half-year and to send them home with pleasant recollections of their last hours together.

The day was a glorious one; the weather was of the kind which, in our climate at least, only falls to our lot in late summer: heaven and earth merged harmoniously with one another, and, glowing wondrously in the sunshine, autumn freshness blended with the blue expanse above. Arrayed in the bright fantastic garb in which, amid the gloomy fashions now reigning, students alone may indulge, we boarded a steamer which was gaily decorated in our honour, and hoisted our flag on its mast. From both banks of the river there came at intervals the sound of signal-guns, fired according to our orders, with the view of acquainting both our host in Rolandseck and the inhabitants in the neighbourhood with our approach. I shall not speak of the noisy journey from the landing-stage, through the excited and expectant little place, nor shall I refer to the esoteric jokes exchanged between ourselves; I also make no mention of a feast which became both wild and noisy, or of an extraordinary musical production in the execution of which, whether as soloists or as chorus, we all ultimately had to share, and which I, as musical adviser of our club, had not only had to rehearse, but was then forced to conduct. Towards the end of this piece, which grew ever wilder and which was sung to ever quicker time, I made a sign to my friend, and just as the last chord rang like a yell through the building, he and I vanished, leaving behind us a raging pandemonium.

In a moment we were in the refreshing and breathless stillness of nature. The shadows were already lengthening, the sun still shone steadily, though it had sunk a good deal in the heavens, and from the green and glittering waves of the Rhine a cool breeze was wafted over our hot faces. Our solemn rite bound us only in so far as the latest hours of the day were concerned, and we therefore determined to employ the last moments of clear daylight by giving ourselves up to one of our many hobbies.

At that time we were passionately fond of pistol-shooting, and both of us in later years found the skill we had acquired as amateurs of great use in our military career. Our club servant happened to know the somewhat distant and elevated spot which we used as a range, and had carried our pistols there in advance. The spot lay near the upper border of the wood which covered the lesser heights behind Rolandseck: it was a small uneven plateau, close to the place we had consecrated in memory of its associations. On a wooded slope alongside of our shooting-range there was a small piece of ground which had been cleared of wood, and which made an ideal halting-place; from it one could get a view of the Rhine over the tops of the trees and the brushwood, so that the beautiful, undulating lines of the Seven Mountains and above all of the Drachenfels bounded the horizon against the group of trees, while in the centre of the bow formed by the glistening Rhine itself the island of Nonnenwörth stood out as if suspended in the river's arms. This was the place which had become sacred to us through the dreams and plans we had had in common, and to which we intended to withdraw, later in the evening,—nay, to which we should be obliged to withdraw, if we wished to close the day in accordance with the law we had imposed on ourselves.

At one end of the little uneven plateau, and not very far away, there stood the mighty trunk of an oak-tree, prominently visible against a background quite bare of trees and consisting merely of low undulating hills in the distance. Working together, we had once carved a pentagram in the side of this tree-trunk. Years of exposure to rain and storm had slightly deepened the channels we had cut, and the figure seemed a welcome target for our pistol-practice. It was already late in the afternoon when we reached our improvised range, and our oak-stump cast a long and attenuated shadow across the barren heath. All was still: thanks to the lofty trees at our feet, we were unable to catch a glimpse of the valley of the Rhine below. The peacefulness of the spot seemed only to intensify the loudness of our pistol-shots—and I had scarcely fired my second barrel at the pentagram when I felt some one lay hold of my arm and noticed that my friend had also some one beside him who had interrupted his loading.

Turning sharply on my heels I found myself face to face with an astonished old gentleman, and felt what must have been a very powerful dog make a lunge at my back. My friend had been approached by a somewhat younger man than I had; but before we could give expression to our surprise the older of the two interlopers burst forth in the following threatening and heated strain: "No! no!" he called to us, "no duels must be fought here, but least of all must you young students fight one. Away with these pistols and compose yourselves. Be reconciled, shake hands! What?—and are you the salt of the earth, the intelligence of the future, the seed of our hopes—and are you not even able to emancipate yourselves from the insane code of honour and its violent regulations? I will not cast any aspersions on your hearts, but your heads certainly do you no credit. You, whose youth is watched over by the wisdom of Greece and Rome, and whose youthful spirits, at the cost of enormous pains, have been flooded with the light of the sages and heroes of antiquity,—can you not refrain from making the code of knightly honour—that is to say, the code of folly and brutality—the guiding principle of your conduct?—Examine it rationally once and for all, and reduce it to plain terms; lay its pitiable narrowness bare, and let it be the touchstone, not of your hearts but of your minds. If you do not regret it then, it will merely show that your head is not fitted for work in a sphere where great gifts of discrimination are needful in order to burst the bonds of prejudice, and where a well-balanced understanding is necessary for the purpose of distinguishing right from wrong, even when the difference between them lies deeply hidden and is not, as in this case, so ridiculously obvious. In that case, therefore, my lads, try to go through life in some other honourable manner; join the army or learn a handicraft that pays its way."

To this rough, though admittedly just, flood of eloquence, we replied with some irritation, interrupting each other continually in so doing: "In the first place, you are mistaken concerning the main point; for we are not here to fight a duel at all; but rather to practise pistol-shooting. Secondly, you do not appear to know how a real duel is conducted;—do you suppose that we should have faced each other in this lonely spot, like two highwaymen, without seconds or doctors, etc. etc.? Thirdly, with regard to the question of duelling, we each have our own opinions, and do not require to be waylaid and surprised by the sort of instruction you may feel disposed to give us."

This reply, which was certainly not polite, made a bad impression upon the old man. At first, when he heard that we were not about to fight a duel, he surveyed us more kindly: but when we reached the last passage of our speech, he seemed so vexed that he growled. When, however, we began to speak of our point of view, he quickly caught hold of his companion, turned sharply round, and cried to us in bitter tones: "People should not have points of view, but thoughts!" And then his companion added: "Be respectful when a man such as this even makes mistakes!"

Meanwhile, my friend, who had reloaded, fired a shot at the pentagram, after having cried: "Look out!" This sudden report behind his back made the old man savage; once more he turned round and looked sourly at my friend, after which he said to his companion in a feeble voice: "What shall we do? These young men will be the death of me with their firing."—"You should know," said the younger man, turning to us, "that your noisy pastimes amount, as it happens on this occasion, to an attempt upon the life of philosophy. You observe this venerable man,—he is in a position to beg you to desist from firing here. And when such a man begs——" "Well, his request is generally granted," the old man interjected, surveying us sternly.

As a matter of fact, we did not know what to make of the whole matter; we could not understand what our noisy pastimes could have in common with philosophy; nor could we see why, out of regard for polite scruples, we should abandon our shooting-range, and at this moment we may have appeared somewhat undecided and perturbed. The companion noticing our momentary discomfiture, proceeded to explain the matter to us.

"We are compelled," he said, "to linger in this immediate neighbourhood for an hour or so; we have a rendezvous here. An eminent friend of this eminent man is to meet us here this evening; and we had actually selected this peaceful spot, with its few benches in the midst of the wood, for the meeting. It would really be most unpleasant if, owing to your continual pistol-practice, we were to be subjected to an unending series of shocks; surely your own feelings will tell you that it is impossible for you to continue your firing when you hear that he who has selected this quiet and isolated place for a meeting with a friend is one of our most eminent philosophers."

This explanation only succeeded in perturbing us the more; for we saw a danger threatening us which was even greater than the loss of our shooting-range, and we asked eagerly, "Where is this quiet spot? Surely not to the left here, in the wood?"

"That is the very place."

"But this evening that place belongs to us," my friend interposed. "We must have it," we cried together.

Our long-projected celebration seemed at that moment more important than all the philosophies of the world, and we gave such vehement and animated utterance to our sentiments that in view of the incomprehensible nature of our claims we must have cut a somewhat ridiculous figure. At any rate, our philosophical interlopers regarded us with expressions of amused inquiry, as if they expected us to proffer some sort of apology. But we were silent, for we wished above all to keep our secret.

Thus we stood facing one another in silence, while the sunset dyed the tree-tops a ruddy gold. The philosopher contemplated the sun, his companion contemplated him, and we turned our eyes towards our nook in the woods which to-day we seemed in such great danger of losing. A feeling of sullen anger took possession of us. What is philosophy, we asked ourselves, if it prevents a man from being by himself or from enjoying the select company of a friend,—in sooth, if it prevents him from becoming a philosopher? For we regarded the celebration of our rite as a thoroughly philosophical performance. In celebrating it we wished to form plans and resolutions for the future, by means of quiet reflections we hoped to light upon an idea which would once again help us to form and gratify our spirit in the future, just as that former idea had done during our boyhood. The solemn act derived its very significance from this resolution, that nothing definite was to be done, we were only to be alone, and to sit still and meditate, as we had done five years before when we had each been inspired with the same thought. It was to be a silent solemnisation, all reminiscence and all future; the present was to be as a hyphen between the two. And fate, now unfriendly, had just stepped into our magic circle—and we knew not how to dismiss her;—the very unusual character of the circumstances filled us with mysterious excitement.

Whilst we stood thus in silence for some time, divided into two hostile groups, the clouds above waxed ever redder and the evening seemed to grow more peaceful and mild; we could almost fancy we heard the regular breathing of nature as she put the final touches to her work of art—the glorious day we had just enjoyed; when, suddenly, the calm evening air was rent by a confused and boisterous cry of joy which seemed to come from the Rhine. A number of voices could be heard in the distance—they were those of our fellow-students who by that time must have taken to the Rhine in small boats. It occurred to us that we should be missed and that we should also miss something: almost simultaneously my friend and I raised our pistols: our shots were echoed back to us, and with their echo there came from the valley the sound of a well-known cry intended as a signal of identification. For our passion for shooting had brought us both repute and ill-repute in our club. At the same time we were conscious that our behaviour towards the silent philosophical couple had been exceptionally ungentlemanly; they had been quietly contemplating us for some time, and when we fired the shock made them draw close up to each other. We hurried up to them, and each in our turn cried out: "Forgive us. That was our last shot, and it was intended for our friends on the Rhine. They have understood us, do you hear? If you insist upon having that place among the trees, grant us at least the permission to recline there also. You will find a number of benches on the spot: we shall not disturb you; we shall sit quite still and shall not utter a word: but it is now past seven o'clock and we *must* go there at once.

"That sounds more mysterious than it is," I added after a pause; "we have made a solemn vow to spend this coming hour on that ground, and there were reasons for the vow. The spot is sacred to us, owing to some pleasant associations, it must also inaugurate a good future for us. We shall therefore endeavour to leave you with no disagreeable recollections of our meeting—even though we have done much to perturb and frighten you."

The philosopher was silent; his companion, however, said: "Our promises and plans unfortunately compel us not only to remain, but also to spend the same hour on the spot you have selected. It is left for us to decide whether fate or perhaps a spirit has been responsible for this extraordinary coincidence."

"Besides, my friend," said the philosopher, "I am not half so displeased with these warlike youngsters as I was. Did you observe how quiet they were a moment ago, when we were contemplating the sun? They neither spoke nor smoked, they stood stone still, I even believe they meditated."

Turning suddenly in our direction, he said: "*Were* you meditating? Just tell me about it as we proceed in the direction of our common trysting-place." We took a few steps together and went down the slope into the warm balmy air of the woods where it was already much darker. On the way my friend openly revealed his thoughts to the philosopher, he confessed how much he had feared that perhaps to-day for the first time a philosopher was about to stand in the way of his philosophising.

The sage laughed. "What? You were afraid a philosopher would prevent your philosophising? This might easily happen: and you have not yet experienced such a thing? Has your university life been free from experience? You surely attend lectures on philosophy?"

This question discomfited us; for, as a matter of fact, there had been no element of philosophy in our education up to that time. In those days, moreover, we fondly imagined that everybody who held the post and possessed the dignity of a philosopher must perforce be one: we were inexperienced and badly informed. We frankly admitted that we had not yet belonged to any philosophical college, but that we would certainly make up for lost time.

"Then what," he asked, "did you mean when you spoke of philosophising?" Said I, "We are at a loss for a definition. But to all intents and purposes we meant this, that we wished to make earnest endeavours to consider the best possible means of becoming men of culture." "That is a good deal and at the same time very little," growled the philosopher; "just you think the matter over. Here are our benches, let us discuss the question exhaustively: I shall not disturb your meditations with regard to how you are to become men of culture. I wish you success and—points of view, as in your duelling questions; brand-new, original, and enlightened points of view. The philosopher does not wish to prevent your philosophising: but refrain at least from disconcerting him with your pistol-shots. Try to imitate the Pythagoreans to-day: they, as servants of a true philosophy, had to remain silent for five years—possibly you may also be able to remain silent for five times fifteen minutes, as servants of your own future culture, about which you seem so concerned."

We had reached our destination: the solemnisation of our rite began. As on the previous occasion, five years ago, the Rhine was once more flowing beneath a light mist, the sky seemed bright and the woods exhaled the same fragrance. We took our places on the farthest corner of the most distant bench; sitting there we were almost concealed, and neither the philosopher nor his companion could see our faces. We were alone: when the sound of the philosopher's voice reached us, it had become so blended with the rustling leaves and with the buzzing murmur of the myriads of living things inhabiting the wooded height, that it almost seemed like the music of nature; as a sound it resembled nothing more than a distant monotonous plaint. We were indeed undisturbed.

Some time elapsed in this way, and while the glow of sunset grew steadily paler the recollection of our youthful undertaking in the cause of culture waxed ever more vivid. It seemed to us as if we owed the greatest debt of gratitude to that little society we had founded; for it had done more than merely supplement our public school training; it had actually been the only fruitful society we had had, and within its frame we even placed our public school life, as a purely isolated factor helping us in our general efforts to attain to culture.

We knew this, that, thanks to our little society, no thought of embracing any particular career had ever entered our minds in those days. The all too frequent exploitation of youth by the State, for its own purposes—that is to say, so that it may rear useful officials as quickly as possible and guarantee their unconditional obedience to it by means of excessively severe examinations—had remained quite foreign to our education. And to show how little we had been actuated by thoughts of utility or by the prospect of speedy advancement and rapid success, on that day we were struck by the comforting consideration that, even then, we had not yet decided what we should be—we had not even troubled ourselves at all on this head. Our little society had sown the seeds of this happy indifference in our souls and for it alone we were prepared to celebrate the anniversary of its foundation with hearty gratitude. I have already pointed out, I think, that in the eyes of the present age, which is so intolerant of anything that is not useful, such purposeless enjoyment of the moment, such a lulling of one's self in the cradle of the present, must seem almost incredible and at all events blameworthy. How useless we were! And how proud we were of being useless! We used even to quarrel with each other as to which of us should have the glory of being the more useless. We wished to attach no importance to anything, to have strong views about nothing, to aim at nothing; we wanted to take no thought for the morrow, and desired no more than to recline comfortably like good-for-nothings on the threshold of the present; and we did—bless us!

—That, ladies and gentlemen, was our standpoint then!—

Absorbed in these reflections, I was just about to give an answer to the question of the future of *our* Educational Institutions in the same self-sufficient way, when it gradually dawned upon me that the "natural music," coming from the philosopher's bench had lost its original character and travelled to us in much more piercing and distinct tones than before. Suddenly I became aware that I was listening, that I was eavesdropping, and was passionately interested, with both ears keenly alive to every sound. I nudged my friend who was evidently somewhat tired, and I whispered: "Don't fall asleep! There is something for us to learn over there. It applies to us, even though it be not meant for us."

For instance, I heard the younger of the two men defending himself with great animation while the philosopher rebuked him with ever increasing vehemence. "You are unchanged," he cried to him, "unfortunately unchanged. It is quite incomprehensible to me how you can still be the same as you were seven years ago, when I saw you for the last time and left you with so much misgiving. I fear I must once again divest you, however reluctantly, of the skin of modern culture which you have donned meanwhile;—and what do I find beneath it? The same immutable 'intelligible' character forsooth, according to Kant; but unfortunately the same unchanged 'intellectual' character, too—which may also be a necessity, though not a comforting one. I ask myself to what purpose have I lived as a philosopher, if, possessed as you are of no mean intelligence and a genuine thirst for knowledge, all the years you have spent in my company have left no deeper impression upon you. At present you are behaving as if you had not even heard the cardinal principle of all culture, which I went to such pains to inculcate upon you during our former intimacy. Tell me,—what was that principle?"

"I remember," replied the scolded pupil, "you used to say no one would strive to attain to culture if he knew how incredibly small the number of really cultured people actually is, and can ever be. And even this number of really cultured people would not be possible if a prodigious multitude, from reasons opposed to their nature and only led on by an alluring delusion, did not devote themselves to education. It were therefore a mistake publicly to reveal the ridiculous disproportion between the number of really cultured people and the enormous magnitude of the educational apparatus. Here lies the whole secret of culture—namely, that an innumerable host of men struggle to achieve it and work hard to that end, ostensibly in their own interests, whereas at bottom it is only in order that it may be possible for the few to attain to it."

"That is the principle," said the philosopher,—"and yet you could so far forget yourself as to believe that you are one of the few? This thought has occurred to you—I can see. That, however, is the result of the worthless character of modern education. The rights of genius are being democratised in order that people may be relieved of the labour of acquiring culture, and their need of it. Every one wants if possible to recline in the shade of the tree planted by genius, and to escape the dreadful necessity of working for him, so that his procreation may be made possible. What? Are you too proud to be a teacher? Do you despise the thronging multitude of learners? Do you speak contemptuously of the teacher's calling? And, aping my mode of life, would you fain live in solitary seclusion, hostilely isolated from that multitude? Do you suppose that you can reach at one bound what I ultimately had to win for myself only after long and determined struggles, in order even to be able to live like a philosopher? And do you not fear that solitude will wreak its vengeance upon you? Just try living the life of a hermit of culture. One must be blessed with overflowing wealth in order to live for the good of all on one's own resources! Extraordinary youngsters!

They felt it incumbent upon them to imitate what is precisely most difficult and most high,—what is possible only to the master, when they, above all, should know how difficult and dangerous this is, and how many excellent gifts may be ruined by attempting it!"

"I will conceal nothing from you, sir," the companion replied. "I have heard too much from your lips at odd times and have been too long in your company to be able to surrender myself entirely to our present system of education and instruction. I am too painfully conscious of the disastrous errors and abuses to which you used to call my attention—though I very well know that I am not strong enough to hope for any success were I to struggle ever so valiantly against them. I was overcome by a feeling of general discouragement; my recourse to solitude was the result neither of pride nor arrogance. I would fain describe to you what I take to be the nature of the educational questions now attracting such enormous and pressing attention. It seemed to me that I must recognise two main directions in the forces at work—two seemingly antagonistic tendencies, equally deleterious in their action, and ultimately combining to produce their results: a striving to achieve the greatest possible *expansion* of education on the one hand, and a tendency to *minimise and weaken* it on the other. The first-named would, for various reasons, spread learning among the greatest number of people; the second would compel education to renounce its highest, noblest and sublimest claims in order to subordinate itself to some other department of life—such as the service of the State.

"I believe I have already hinted at the quarter in which the cry for the greatest possible expansion of education is most loudly raised. This expansion belongs to the most beloved of the dogmas of modern political economy. As much knowledge and education as possible; therefore the greatest possible supply and demand—hence as much happiness as possible:—that is the formula. In this case utility is made the object and goal of education,—utility in the sense of gain—the greatest possible pecuniary gain. In the quarter now under consideration culture would be defined as that point of vantage which enables one to 'keep in the van of one's age,' from which one can see all the easiest and best roads to wealth, and with which one controls all the means of communication between men and nations. The purpose of education, according to this scheme, would be to rear the most 'current' men possible,—'current' being used here in the sense in which it is applied to the coins of the realm. The greater the number of such men, the happier a nation will be; and this precisely is the purpose of our modern educational institutions: to help every one, as far as his nature will allow, to become 'current'; to develop him so that his particular degree of knowledge and science may yield him the greatest possible amount of happiness and pecuniary gain. Every one must be able to form some sort of estimate of himself; he must know how much he may reasonably expect from life. The 'bond between intelligence and property' which this point of view postulates has almost the force of a moral principle. In this quarter all culture is loathed which isolates, which sets goals beyond gold and gain, and which requires time: it is customary to dispose of such eccentric tendencies in education as systems of 'Higher Egotism,' or of 'Immoral Culture—Epicureanism.' According to the morality reigning here, the demands are quite different; what is required above all is 'rapid education,' so that a money-earning creature may be produced with all speed; there is even a desire to make this education so thorough that a creature may be reared that will be able to earn a *great deal* of money. Men are allowed only the precise amount of culture which is compatible with the interests of gain; but that amount, at least, is expected from them. In short: mankind has a necessary right to happiness on earth—that is why culture is necessary—but on that account alone!"

"I must just say something here," said the philosopher. "In the case of the view you have described so clearly, there arises the great and awful danger that at some time or other the great masses may overleap the middle classes and spring headlong into this earthly bliss. That is what is now called 'the social question.' It might seem to these masses that education for the greatest number of men was only a means to the earthly bliss of the few: the 'greatest possible expansion of education' so enfeebles education that it can no longer confer privileges or inspire respect. The most general form of culture is simply barbarism. But I do not wish to interrupt your discussion."

The companion continued: "There are yet other reasons, besides this beloved economical dogma, for the expansion of education that is being striven after so valiantly everywhere. In some countries the fear of religious oppression is so general, and the dread of its results so marked, that people in all classes of society long for culture and eagerly absorb those elements of it which are supposed to scatter the religious instincts. Elsewhere the State, in its turn, strives here and there for its own preservation, after the greatest possible expansion of education, because it always feels strong enough to bring the most determined emancipation, resulting from culture, under its yoke, and readily approves of everything which tends to extend culture, provided that it be of service to its officials or soldiers, but in the main to itself, in its competition with other nations. In this case, the foundations of a State must be sufficiently broad and firm to constitute a fitting counterpart to the complicated arches of culture which it supports, just as in the first case the traces of some former religious tyranny must still be felt for a people to be driven to such desperate remedies. Thus, wherever I hear the masses raise the cry for an expansion of education, I am wont to ask myself whether it is stimulated by a greedy lust of gain and property, by the memory of a former religious persecution, or by the prudent egotism of the State itself.

"On the other hand, it seemed to me that there was yet another tendency, not so clamorous, perhaps, but quite as forcible, which, hailing from various quarters, was animated by a different desire,—the desire to minimise and weaken education.

"In all cultivated circles people are in the habit of whispering to one another words something after this style: that it is a general fact that, owing to the present frantic exploitation of the scholar in the service of his science, his *education* becomes every day more accidental and more uncertain. For the study of science has been extended to such interminable lengths that he who, though not exceptionally gifted, yet possesses fair abilities, will need to devote himself exclusively to one branch and ignore all others if he ever wish to achieve anything in his work. Should he then elevate himself above the herd by means of his speciality, he still remains one of them in regard to all else,—that is to say, in regard to all the most important things in life. Thus, a specialist in science gets to resemble nothing so much as a factory workman who spends his whole life in turning one particular screw or handle on a certain instrument or machine, at which occupation he acquires the most consummate skill. In Germany, where we know how to drape such painful facts with the glorious garments of fancy, this narrow specialisation on the part of our learned men is even admired, and their ever greater deviation from the path of true culture is regarded as a moral phenomenon. 'Fidelity in small things,' 'dogged faithfulness,' become expressions of highest eulogy, and the lack of culture outside the speciality is flaunted abroad as a sign of noble sufficiency.

"For centuries it has been an understood thing that one alluded to scholars alone when one spoke of cultured men; but experience tells us that it would be difficult to find any necessary relation between the two classes to-day. For at present the exploitation of a man for the purpose of science is accepted everywhere without the slightest scruple. Who still ventures to ask, What may be the value of a science which consumes its minions in this vampire fashion? The division of labour in science is practically struggling towards the same goal which religions in certain parts of the world are consciously striving after,—that is to say, towards the decrease and even the destruction of learning. That, however, which, in the case of certain religions, is a perfectly justifiable aim, both in regard to their origin and their history, can only amount to self-immolation when transferred to the realm of science. In all matters of a general and serious nature, and above all, in regard to the highest philosophical problems, we have now already reached a point at which the scientific man, as such, is no longer allowed to speak. On the other hand, that adhesive and tenacious stratum which has now filled up the interstices between the sciences—Journalism—believes it has a mission to fulfil here, and this it does, according to its own particular lights—that is to say, as its name implies, after the fashion of a day-labourer.

"It is precisely in journalism that the two tendencies combine and become one. The expansion and the diminution of education here join hands. The newspaper actually steps into the place of culture, and he who, even as a scholar, wishes to voice any claim for education, must avail himself of this viscous stratum of communication which cements the seams between all forms of life, all classes, all arts, and all sciences, and which is as firm and reliable as news paper is, as a rule. In the newspaper the peculiar educational aims of the present culminate, just as the journalist, the servant of the moment, has stepped into the place of the genius, of the leader for all time, of the deliverer from the tyranny of the moment. Now, tell me, distinguished master, what hopes could I still have in a struggle against the general topsy-turvification of all genuine aims for education; with what courage can I, a single teacher, step forward, when I know that the moment any seeds of real culture are sown, they will be mercilessly crushed by the roller of this pseudo-culture? Imagine how useless the most energetic work on the part of the individual teacher must be, who would fain lead a pupil back into the distant and evasive Hellenic world and to the real home of culture, when in less than an hour, that same pupil will have recourse to a newspaper, the latest novel, or one of those learned books, the very style of which already bears the revolting impress of modern barbaric culture——"

“Now, silence a minute!” interjected the philosopher in a strong and sympathetic voice. “I understand you now, and ought never to have spoken so crossly to you. You are altogether right, save in your despair. I shall now proceed to say a few words of consolation.”

Second Lecture.

(Delivered on the 6th of February 1872.)

Ladies and Gentlemen,—Those among you whom I now have the pleasure of addressing for the first time and whose only knowledge of my first lecture has been derived from reports will, I hope, not mind being introduced here into the middle of a dialogue which I had begun to recount on the last occasion, and the last points of which I must now recall. The philosopher's young companion was just pleading openly and confidentially with his distinguished tutor, and apologising for having so far renounced his calling as a teacher in order to spend his days in comfortless solitude. No suspicion of superciliousness or arrogance had induced him to form this resolve.

"I have heard too much from your lips at various times," the straightforward pupil said, "and have been too long in your company, to surrender myself blindly to our present systems of education and instruction. I am too painfully conscious of the disastrous errors and abuses to which you were wont to call my attention; and yet I know that I am far from possessing the requisite strength to meet with success, however valiantly I might struggle to shatter the bulwarks of this would-be culture. I was overcome by a general feeling of depression: my recourse to solitude was not arrogance or superciliousness." Whereupon, to account for his behaviour, he described the general character of modern educational methods so vividly that the philosopher could not help interrupting him in a voice full of sympathy, and crying words of comfort to him.

"Now, silence for a minute, my poor friend," he cried; "I can more easily understand you now, and should not have lost my patience with you. You are altogether right, save in your despair. I shall now proceed to say a few words of comfort to you. How long do you suppose the state of education in the schools of our time, which seems to weigh so heavily upon you, will last? I shall not conceal my views on this point from you: its time is over; its days are counted. The first who will dare to be quite straightforward in this respect will hear his honesty re-echoed back to him by thousands of courageous souls. For, at bottom, there is a tacit understanding between the more nobly gifted and more warmly disposed men of the present day. Every one of them knows what he has had to suffer from the condition of culture in schools; every one of them would fain protect his offspring from the need of enduring similar drawbacks, even though he himself was compelled to submit to them. If these feelings are never quite honestly expressed, however, it is owing to a sad want of spirit among modern pedagogues. These lack real initiative; there are too few practical men among them—that is to say, too few who happen to have good and new ideas, and who know that real genius and the real practical mind must necessarily come together in the same individuals, whilst the sober practical men have no ideas and therefore fall short in practice.

"Let any one examine the pedagogic literature of the present; he who is not shocked at its utter poverty of spirit and its ridiculously awkward antics is beyond being spoiled. Here our philosophy must not begin with wonder but with dread; he who feels no dread at this point must be asked not to meddle with pedagogic questions. The reverse, of course, has been the rule up to the present; those who were terrified ran away filled with embarrassment as you did, my poor friend, while the sober and fearless ones spread their heavy hands over the most delicate technique that has ever existed in art—over the technique of education. This, however, will not be possible much longer; at some time or other the upright man will appear, who will not only have the good ideas I speak of, but who in order to work at their realisation, will dare to break with all that exists at present: he may by means of a wonderful example achieve what the broad hands, hitherto active, could not even imitate—then people will everywhere begin to draw comparisons; then men will at least be able to perceive a contrast and will be in a position to reflect upon its causes, whereas, at present, so many still believe, in perfect good faith, that heavy hands are a necessary factor in pedagogic work."

"My dear master," said the younger man, "I wish you could point to one single example which would assist me in seeing the soundness of the hopes which you so heartily raise in me. We are both acquainted with public schools; do you think, for instance, that in respect of these institutions anything may be done by means of honesty and good and new ideas to abolish the tenacious and antiquated customs now extant? In this quarter, it seems to me, the battering-rams of an attacking party will have to meet with no solid wall, but with the most fatal of stolid and slippery principles. The leader of the assault has no visible and tangible opponent to crush, but rather a creature in disguise that can transform itself into a hundred different shapes and, in each of these, slip out of his grasp, only in order to reappear and to confound its enemy by cowardly surrenders and feigned retreats. It was precisely the public schools which drove me into despair and solitude, simply because I feel that if the struggle here leads to victory all other educational institutions must give in; but that, if the reformer be forced to abandon his cause here, he may as well give up all hope in regard to every other scholastic question. Therefore, dear master, enlighten me concerning the public schools; what can we hope for in the way of their abolition or reform?"

"I also hold the question of public schools to be as important as you do," the philosopher replied. "All other educational institutions must fix their aims in accordance with those of the public school system; whatever errors of judgment it may suffer from, they suffer from also, and if it were ever purified and rejuvenated, they would be purified and rejuvenated too. The universities can no longer lay claim to this importance as centres of influence, seeing that, as they now stand, they are at least, in one important aspect, only a kind of annex to the public school system, as I shall shortly point out to you. For the moment, let us consider, together, what to my mind constitutes the very hopeful struggle of the two possibilities: *either* that the motley and evasive spirit of public schools which has hitherto been fostered, will completely vanish, or that it will have to be completely purified and rejuvenated. And in order that I may not shock you with general propositions, let us first try to recall one of those public school experiences which we have all had, and from which we have all suffered. Under severe examination what, as a matter of fact, is the present *system of teaching German* in public schools?

"I shall first of all tell you what it should be. Everybody speaks and writes German as thoroughly badly as it is just possible to do so in an age of newspaper German: that is why the growing youth who happens to be both noble and gifted has to be taken by force and put under the glass shade of good taste and of severe linguistic discipline. If this is not possible, I would prefer in future that Latin be spoken; for I am ashamed of a language so bungled and vitiated.

"What would be the duty of a higher educational institution, in this respect, if not this—namely, with authority and dignified severity to put youths, neglected, as far as their own language is concerned, on the right path, and to cry to them: 'Take your own language seriously! He who does not regard this matter as a sacred duty does not possess even the germ of a higher culture. From your attitude in this matter, from your treatment of your mother-tongue, we can judge how highly or how lowly you esteem art, and to what extent you are related to it. If you notice no physical loathing in yourselves when you meet with certain words and tricks of speech in our journalistic jargon, cease from striving after culture; for here in your immediate vicinity, at every moment of your life, while you are either speaking or writing, you have a touchstone for testing how difficult, how stupendous, the task of the cultured man is, and how very improbable it must be that many of you will ever attain to culture.'

"In accordance with the spirit of this address, the teacher of German at a public school would be forced to call his pupil's attention to thousands of details, and with the absolute certainty of good taste, to forbid their using such words and expressions, for instance, as: '*beanspruchen,*' '*vereinnahmen,*' '*einer Sache Rechnung tragen,*' '*die Initiative ergreifen,*' '*selbstverständlich,*'[3] etc., *cum tædio in infinitum*. The same teacher would also have to take our classical authors and show, line for line, how carefully and with what precision every expression has to be chosen when a writer has the correct feeling in his heart and has before his eyes a perfect conception of all he is writing. He would necessarily urge his pupils, time and again, to express the same thought ever more happily; nor would he have to abate in rigour until the less gifted in his class had contracted an unholy fear of their language, and the others had developed great enthusiasm for it.

"Here then is a task for so-called 'formal' education[4] [the education tending to develop the mental faculties, as opposed to 'material' education,[5]

[3] It is not practicable to translate these German solecisms by similar instances of English solecisms. The reader who is interested in the subject will find plenty of material in a book like the Oxford *King's English.*

[4] German: *Formelle Bildung.*

[5] German: *Materielle Bildung.*

which is intended to deal only with the acquisition of facts, *e.g.* history, mathematics, etc.], and one of the utmost value: but what do we find in the public school—that is to say, in the head-quarters of formal education? He who understands how to apply what he has heard here will also know what to think of the modern public school as a so-called educational institution. He will discover, for instance, that the public school, according to its fundamental principles, does not educate for the purposes of culture, but for the purposes of scholarship; and, further, that of late it seems to have adopted a course which indicates rather that it has even discarded scholarship in favour of journalism as the object of its exertions. This can be clearly seen from the way in which German is taught.

"Instead of that purely practical method of instruction by which the teacher accustoms his pupils to severe self-discipline in their own language, we find everywhere the rudiments of a historico-scholastic method of teaching the mother-tongue: that is to say, people deal with it as if it were a dead language and as if the present and future were under no obligations to it whatsoever. The historical method has become so universal in our time, that even the living body of the language is sacrificed for the sake of anatomical study. But this is precisely where culture begins—namely, in understanding how to treat the quick as something vital, and it is here too that the mission of the cultured teacher begins: in suppressing the urgent claims of 'historical interests' wherever it is above all necessary to *do* properly and not merely to *know* properly. Our mother-tongue, however, is a domain in which the pupil must learn how to *do* properly, and to this practical end, alone, the teaching of German is essential in our scholastic establishments. The historical method may certainly be a considerably easier and more comfortable one for the teacher; it also seems to be compatible with a much lower grade of ability and, in general, with a smaller display of energy and will on his part. But we shall find that this observation holds good in every department of pedagogic life: the simpler and more comfortable method always masquerades in the disguise of grand pretensions and stately titles; the really practical side, the *doing*, which should belong to culture and which, at bottom, is the more difficult side, meets only with disfavour and contempt. That is why the honest man must make himself and others quite clear concerning this *quid pro quo*.

"Now, apart from these learned incentives to a study of the language, what is there besides which the German teacher is wont to offer? How does he reconcile the spirit of his school with the spirit of the *few* that Germany can claim who are really cultured,—*i.e.* with the spirit of its classical poets and artists? This is a dark and thorny sphere, into which one cannot even bear a light without dread; but even here we shall conceal nothing from ourselves; for sooner or later the whole of it will have to be reformed. In the public school, the repulsive impress of our æsthetic journalism is stamped upon the still unformed minds of youths. Here, too, the teacher sows the seeds of that crude and wilful misinterpretation of the classics, which later on disports itself as art-criticism, and which is nothing but bumptious barbarity. Here the pupils learn to speak of our unique *Schiller* with the superciliousness of prigs; here they are taught to smile at the noblest and most German of his works—at the Marquis of Posa, at Max and Thekla—at these smiles German genius becomes incensed and a worthier posterity will blush.

"The last department in which the German teacher in a public school is at all active, which is often regarded as his sphere of highest activity, and is here and there even considered the pinnacle of public school education, is the so-called *German composition.* Owing to the very fact that in this department it is almost always the most gifted pupils who display the greatest eagerness, it ought to have been made clear how dangerously stimulating, precisely here, the task of the teacher must be. *German composition* makes an appeal to the individual, and the more strongly a pupil is conscious of his various qualities, the more personally will he do his *German composition.* This 'personal doing' is urged on with yet an additional fillip in some public schools by the choice of the subject, the strongest proof of which is, in my opinion, that even in the lower classes the non-pedagogic subject is set, by means of which the pupil is led to give a description of his life and of his development. Now, one has only to read the titles of the compositions set in a large number of public schools to be convinced that probably the large majority of pupils have to suffer their whole lives, through no fault of their own, owing to this premature demand for personal work—for the unripe procreation of thoughts. And how often are not all a man's subsequent literary performances but a sad result of this pedagogic original sin against the intellect!

"Let us only think of what takes place at such an age in the production of such work. It is the first individual creation; the still undeveloped powers tend for the first time to crystallise; the staggering sensation produced by the demand for self-reliance imparts a seductive charm to these early performances, which is not only quite new, but which never returns. All the daring of nature is hauled out of its depths; all vanities—no longer constrained by mighty barriers—are allowed for the first time to assume a literary form: the young man, from that time forward, feels as if he had reached his consummation as a being not only able, but actually invited, to speak and to converse. The subject he selects obliges him either to express his judgment upon certain poetical works, to class historical persons together in a description of character, to discuss serious ethical problems quite independently, or even to turn the searchlight inwards, to throw its rays upon his own development and to make a critical report of himself: in short, a whole world of reflection is spread out before the astonished young man who, until then, had been almost unconscious, and is delivered up to him to be judged.

"Now let us try to picture the teacher's usual attitude towards these first highly influential examples of original composition. What does he hold to be most reprehensible in this class of work? What does he call his pupil's attention to?—To all excess in form or thought—that is to say, to all that which, at their age, is essentially characteristic and individual. Their really independent traits which, in response to this very premature excitation, can manifest themselves only in awkwardness, crudeness, and grotesque features,—in short, their individuality is reproved and rejected by the teacher in favour of an unoriginal decent average. On the other hand, uniform mediocrity gets peevish praise; for, as a rule, it is just the class of work likely to bore the teacher thoroughly.

"There may still be men who recognise a most absurd and most dangerous element of the public school curriculum in the whole farce of this German composition. Originality is demanded here: but the only shape in which it can manifest itself is rejected, and the 'formal' education that the system takes for granted is attained to only by a very limited number of men who complete it at a ripe age. Here everybody without exception is regarded as gifted for literature and considered as capable of holding opinions concerning the most important questions and people, whereas the one aim which proper education should most zealously strive to achieve would be the suppression of all ridiculous claims to independent judgment, and the inculcation upon young men of obedience to the sceptre of genius. Here a pompous form of diction is taught in an age when every spoken or written word is a piece of barbarism. Now let us consider, besides, the danger of arousing the self-complacency which is so easily awakened in youths; let us think how their vanity must be flattered when they see their literary reflection for the first time in the mirror. Who, having seen all these effects at *one* glance, could any longer doubt whether all the faults of our public, literary, and artistic life were not stamped upon every fresh generation by the system we are examining: hasty and vain production, the disgraceful manufacture of books; complete want of style; the crude, characterless, or sadly swaggering method of expression; the loss of every æsthetic canon; the voluptuousness of anarchy and chaos—in short, the literary peculiarities of both our journalism and our scholarship.

"None but the very fewest are aware that, among many thousands, perhaps only *one* is justified in describing himself as literary, and that all others who at their own risk try to be so deserve to be met with Homeric laughter by all competent men as a reward for every sentence they have ever had printed;—for it is truly a spectacle meet for the gods to see a literary Hephaistos limping forward who would pretend to help us to something. To educate men to earnest and inexorable habits and views, in this respect, should be the highest aim of all mental training, whereas the general *laisser aller* of the 'fine personality' can be nothing else than the hall-mark of barbarism. From what I have said, however, it must be clear that, at least in the teaching of German, no thought is given to culture; something quite different is in view,—namely, the production of the afore-mentioned 'free personality.' And so long as German public schools prepare the road for outrageous and irresponsible scribbling, so long as they do not regard the immediate and practical discipline of speaking and writing as their most holy duty, so long as they treat the mother-tongue as if it were only a necessary evil or a dead body, I shall not regard these institutions as belonging to real culture.

"In regard to the language, what is surely least noticeable is any trace of the influence of *classical examples*: that is why, on the strength of this consideration alone, the so-called 'classical education' which is supposed to be provided by our public school, strikes me as something exceedingly doubtful and confused. For how could anybody, after having cast one glance at those examples, fail to see the great earnestness with which the Greek and the Roman regarded and treated his language, from his youth onwards—how is it possible to mistake one's example on a point like this one?—provided, of course, that the classical Hellenic and Roman world really did hover before the educational plan of our public schools as the highest and most instructive of all morals—a fact I feel very much inclined to doubt. The claim put forward by public schools concerning the 'classical education' they provide seems to be more an awkward evasion than anything else; it is used whenever there is any question raised as to the competency of the public schools to impart culture and to educate. Classical education, indeed! It sounds so dignified! It confounds the aggressor and staves off the assault—for who could see to the bottom of this bewildering formula all at once? And this has long been the customary strategy of the public school: from whichever side the war-cry may come, it writes upon its shield—not overloaded with honours—one of those confusing catchwords, such as: 'classical education,' 'formal education,' 'scientific education':—three glorious things which are, however, unhappily at loggerheads, not only with themselves but among themselves, and are such that, if they were compulsorily brought together, would perforce bring forth a culture-monster. For a 'classical education' is something so unheard of, difficult and rare, and exacts such complicated talent, that only ingenuousness or impudence could put it forward as an attainable goal in our public schools. The words: 'formal education' belong to that crude kind of unphilosophical phraseology which one should do one's utmost to get rid of; for there is no such thing as 'the opposite of formal education.' And he who regards 'scientific education' as the object of a public school thereby sacrifices 'classical education' and the so-called 'formal education,' at one stroke, as the scientific man and the cultured man belong to two different spheres which, though coming together at times in the same individual, are never reconciled.

"If we compare all three of these would-be aims of the public school with the actual facts to be observed in the present method of teaching German, we see immediately what they really amount to in practice,—that is to say, only to subterfuges for use in the fight and struggle for existence and, often enough, mere means wherewith to bewilder an opponent. For we are unable to detect any single feature in this teaching of German which in any way recalls the example of classical antiquity and its glorious methods of training in languages. 'Formal education,' however, which is supposed to be achieved by this method of teaching German, has been shown to be wholly at the pleasure of the 'free personality,' which is as good as saying that it is barbarism and anarchy. And as for the preparation in science, which is one of the consequences of this teaching, our Germanists will have to determine, in all justice, how little these learned beginnings in public schools have contributed to the splendour of their sciences, and how much the personality of individual university professors has done so.—Put briefly: the public school has hitherto neglected its most important and most urgent duty towards the very beginning of all real culture, which is the mother-tongue; but in so doing it has lacked the natural, fertile soil for all further efforts at culture. For only by means of stern, artistic, and careful discipline and habit, in a language, can the correct feeling for the greatness of our classical writers be strengthened. Up to the present their recognition by the public schools has been owing almost solely to the doubtful æsthetic hobbies of a few teachers or to the massive effects of certain of their tragedies and novels. But everybody should, himself, be aware of the difficulties of the language: he should have learnt them from experience: after long seeking and struggling he must reach the path our great poets trod in order to be able to realise how lightly and beautifully they trod it, and how stiffly and swaggeringly the others follow at their heels.

"Only by means of such discipline can the young man acquire that physical loathing for the beloved and much-admired 'elegance' of style of our newspaper manufacturers and novelists, and for the 'ornate style' of our literary men; by it alone is he irrevocably elevated at a stroke above a whole host of absurd questions and scruples, such, for instance, as whether Auerbach and Gutzkow are really poets, for his disgust at both will be so great that he will be unable to read them any longer, and thus the problem will be solved for him. Let no one imagine that it is an easy matter to develop this feeling to the extent necessary in order to have this physical loathing; but let no one hope to reach sound æsthetic judgments along any other road than the thorny one of language, and by this I do not mean philological research, but self-discipline in one's mother-tongue.

"Everybody who is in earnest in this matter will have the same sort of experience as the recruit in the army who is compelled to learn walking after having walked almost all his life as a dilettante or empiricist. It is a hard time: one almost fears that the tendons are going to snap and one ceases to hope that the artificial and consciously acquired movements and positions of the feet will ever be carried out with ease and comfort. It is painful to see how awkwardly and heavily one foot is set before the other, and one dreads that one may not only be unable to learn the new way of walking, but that one will forget how to walk at all. Then it suddenly become noticeable that a new habit and a second nature have been born of the practised movements, and that the assurance and strength of the old manner of walking returns with a little more grace: at this point one begins to realise how difficult walking is, and one feels in a position to laugh at the untrained empiricist or the elegant dilettante. Our 'elegant' writers, as their style shows, have never learnt 'walking' in this sense, and in our public schools, as our other writers show, no one learns walking either. Culture begins, however, with the correct movement of the language: and once it has properly begun, it begets that physical sensation in the presence of 'elegant' writers which is known by the name of 'loathing.'

"We recognise the fatal consequences of our present public schools, in that they are unable to inculcate severe and genuine culture, which should consist above all in obedience and habituation; and that, at their best, they much more often achieve a result by stimulating and kindling scientific tendencies, is shown by the hand which is so frequently seen uniting scholarship and barbarous taste, science and journalism. In a very large majority of cases to-day we can observe how sadly our scholars fall short of the standard of culture which the efforts of Goethe, Schiller, Lessing, and Winckelmann established; and this falling short shows itself precisely in the egregious errors which the men we speak of are exposed to, equally among literary historians—whether Gervinus or Julian Schmidt—as in any other company; everywhere, indeed, where men and women converse. It shows itself most frequently and painfully, however, in pedagogic spheres, in the literature of public schools. It can be proved that the only value that these men have in a real educational establishment has not been mentioned, much less generally recognised for half a century: their value as preparatory leaders and mystogogues of classical culture, guided by whose hands alone can the correct road leading to antiquity be found.

"Every so-called classical education can have but one natural starting-point—an artistic, earnest, and exact familiarity with the use of the mother-tongue: this, together with the secret of form, however, one can seldom attain to of one's own accord, almost everybody requires those great leaders and tutors and must place himself in their hands. There is, however, no such thing as a classical education that could grow without this inferred love of form. Here, where the power of discerning form and barbarity gradually awakens, there appear the pinions which bear one to the only real home of culture—ancient Greece. If with the solitary help of those pinions we sought to reach those far-distant and diamond-studded walls encircling the stronghold of Hellenism, we should certainly not get very far; once more, therefore, we need the same leaders and tutors, our German classical writers, that we may be borne up, too, by the wing-strokes of their past endeavours—to the land of yearning, to Greece.

"Not a suspicion of this possible relationship between our classics and classical education seems to have pierced the antique walls of public schools. Philologists seem much more eagerly engaged in introducing Homer and Sophocles to the young souls of their pupils, in their own style, calling the result simply by the unchallenged euphemism: 'classical education.' Let every one's own experience tell him what he had of Homer and Sophocles at the hands of such eager teachers. It is in this department that the greatest number of deepest deceptions occur, and whence misunderstandings are inadvertently spread. In German public schools I have never yet found a trace of what might really be called 'classical education,' and there is nothing surprising in this when one thinks of the way in which these institutions have emancipated themselves from German classical writers and the discipline of the German language. Nobody reaches antiquity by means of a leap into the dark, and yet the whole method of treating ancient writers in schools, the plain commentating and paraphrasing of our philological teachers, amounts to nothing more than a leap into the dark.

"The feeling for classical Hellenism is, as a matter of fact, such an exceptional outcome of the most energetic fight for culture and artistic talent that the public school could only have professed to awaken this feeling owing to a very crude misunderstanding. In what age? In an age which is led about blindly by the most sensational desires of the day, and which is not aware of the fact that, once that feeling for Hellenism is roused, it immediately becomes aggressive and must express itself by indulging in an incessant war with the so-called culture of the present. For the public school boy of to-day, the Hellenes as Hellenes are dead: yes, he gets some enjoyment out of Homer, but a novel by Spielhagen interests him much more: yes, he swallows Greek tragedy and comedy with a certain relish, but a thoroughly modern drama, like Freitag's 'Journalists,' moves him in quite another fashion. In regard to all ancient authors he is rather inclined to speak after the manner of the æsthete, Hermann Grimm, who, on one occasion, at the end of a tortuous essay on the Venus of Milo, asks himself:

'What does this goddess's form mean to me? Of what use are the thoughts she suggests to me? Orestes and Œdipus, Iphigenia and Antigone, what have they in common with my heart?'—No, my dear public school boy, the Venus of Milo does not concern you in any way, and concerns your teacher just as little—and that is the misfortune, that is the secret of the modern public school. Who will conduct you to the land of culture, if your leaders are blind and assume the position of seers notwithstanding? Which of you will ever attain to a true feeling for the sacred seriousness of art, if you are systematically spoiled, and taught to stutter independently instead of being taught to speak; to æstheticise on your own account, when you ought to be taught to approach works of art almost piously; to philosophise without assistance, while you ought to be compelled to *listen* to great thinkers. All this with the result that you remain eternally at a distance from antiquity and become the servants of the day.

"At all events, the most wholesome feature of our modern institutions is to be found in the earnestness with which the Latin and Greek languages are studied over a long course of years. In this way boys learn to respect a grammar, lexicons, and a language that conforms to fixed rules; in this department of public school work there is an exact knowledge of what constitutes a fault, and no one is troubled with any thought of justifying himself every minute by appealing (as in the case of modern German) to various grammatical and orthographical vagaries and vicious forms. If only this respect for language did not hang in the air so, like a theoretical burden which one is pleased to throw off the moment one turns to one's mother-tongue! More often than not, the classical master makes pretty short work of the mother-tongue; from the outset he treats it as a department of knowledge in which one is allowed that indolent ease with which the German treats everything that belongs to his native soil. The splendid practice afforded by translating from one language into another, which so improves and fertilises one's artistic feeling for one's own tongue, is, in the case of German, never conducted with that fitting categorical strictness and dignity which would be above all necessary in dealing with an undisciplined language. Of late, exercises of this kind have tended to decrease ever more and more: people are satisfied to *know* the foreign classical tongues, they would scorn being able to *apply* them.

"Here one gets another glimpse of the scholarly tendency of public schools: a phenomenon which throws much light upon the object which once animated them,—that is to say, the serious desire to cultivate the pupil. This belonged to the time of our great poets, those few really cultured Germans,—the time when the magnificent Friedrich August Wolf directed the new stream of classical thought, introduced from Greece and Rome by those men, into the heart of the public schools. Thanks to his bold start, a new order of public schools was established, which thenceforward was not to be merely a nursery for science, but, above all, the actual consecrated home of all higher and nobler culture.

"Of the many necessary measures which this change called into being, some of the most important have been transferred with lasting success to the modern regulations of public schools: the most important of all, however, did not succeed—the one demanding that the teacher, also, should be consecrated to the new spirit, so that the aim of the public school has meanwhile considerably departed from the original plan laid down by Wolf, which was the cultivation of the pupil. The old estimate of scholarship and scholarly culture, as an absolute, which Wolf overcame, seems after a slow and spiritless struggle rather to have taken the place of the culture-principle of more recent introduction, and now claims its former exclusive rights, though not with the same frankness, but disguised and with features veiled. And the reason why it was impossible to make public schools fall in with the magnificent plan of classical culture lay in the un-German, almost foreign or cosmopolitan nature of these efforts in the cause of education: in the belief that it was possible to remove the native soil from under a man's feet and that he should still remain standing; in the illusion that people can spring direct, without bridges, into the strange Hellenic world, by abjuring German and the German mind in general.

"Of course one must know how to trace this Germanic spirit to its lair beneath its many modern dressings, or even beneath heaps of ruins; one must love it so that one is not ashamed of it in its stunted form, and one must above all be on one's guard against confounding it with what now disports itself proudly as 'Up-to-date German culture.' The German spirit is very far from being on friendly times with this up-to-date culture: and precisely in those spheres where the latter complains of a lack of culture the real German spirit has survived, though perhaps not always with a graceful, but more often an ungraceful, exterior. On the other hand, that which now grandiloquently assumes the title of 'German culture' is a sort of cosmopolitan aggregate, which bears the same relation to the German spirit as Journalism does to Schiller or Meyerbeer to Beethoven: here the strongest influence at work is the fundamentally and thoroughly un-German civilisation of France, which is aped neither with talent nor with taste, and the imitation of which gives the society, the press, the art, and the literary style of Germany their pharisaical character. Naturally the copy nowhere produces the really artistic effect which the original, grown out of the heart of Roman civilisation, is able to produce almost to this day in France. Let any one who wishes to see the full force of this contrast compare our most noted novelists with the less noted ones of France or Italy: he will recognise in both the same doubtful tendencies and aims, as also the same still more doubtful means, but in France he will find them coupled with artistic earnestness, at least with grammatical purity, and often with beauty, while in their every feature he will recognise the echo of a corresponding social culture. In Germany, on the other hand, they will strike him as unoriginal, flabby, filled with dressing-gown thoughts and expressions, unpleasantly spread out, and therewithal possessing no background of social form. At the most, owing to their scholarly mannerisms and display of knowledge, he will be reminded of the fact that in Latin countries it is the artistically-trained man, and that in Germany it is the abortive scholar, who becomes a journalist. With this would-be German and thoroughly unoriginal culture, the German can nowhere reckon upon victory: the Frenchman and the Italian will always get the better of him in this respect, while, in regard to the clever imitation of a foreign culture, the Russian, above all, will always be his superior.

"We are therefore all the more anxious to hold fast to that German spirit which revealed itself in the German Reformation, and in German music, and which has shown its enduring and genuine strength in the enormous courage and severity of German philosophy and in the loyalty of the German soldier, which has been tested quite recently. From it we expect a victory over that 'up-to-date' pseudo-culture which is now the fashion. What we should hope for the future is that schools may draw the real school of culture into this struggle, and kindle the flame of enthusiasm in the younger generation, more particularly in public schools, for that which is truly German; and in this way so-called classical education will resume its natural place and recover its one possible starting-point.

"A thorough reformation and purification of the public school can only be the outcome of a profound and powerful reformation and purification of the German spirit. It is a very complex and difficult task to find the border-line which joins the heart of the Germanic spirit with the genius of Greece. Not, however, before the noblest needs of genuine German genius snatch at the hand of this genius of Greece as at a firm post in the torrent of barbarity, not before a devouring yearning for this genius of Greece takes possession of German genius, and not before that view of the Greek home, on which Schiller and Goethe, after enormous exertions, were able to feast their eyes, has become the Mecca of the best and most gifted men, will the aim of classical education in public schools acquire any definition; and they at least will not be to blame who teach ever so little science and learning in public schools, in order to keep a definite and at the same time ideal aim in their eyes, and to rescue their pupils from that glistening phantom which now allows itself to be called 'culture' and 'education.' This is the sad plight of the public school of to-day: the narrowest views remain in a certain measure right, because no one seems able to reach or, at least, to indicate the spot where all these views culminate in error."

"No one?" the philosopher's pupil inquired with a slight quaver in his voice; and both men were silent.

Third Lecture.

(Delivered on the 27th of February 1872.)

Ladies and Gentlemen,—At the close of my last lecture, the conversation to which I was a listener, and the outlines of which, as I clearly recollect them, I am now trying to lay before you, was interrupted by a long and solemn pause. Both the philosopher and his companion sat silent, sunk in deep dejection: the peculiarly critical state of that important educational institution, the German public school, lay upon their souls like a heavy burden, which one single, well-meaning individual is not strong enough to remove, and the multitude, though strong, not well meaning enough.

Our solitary thinkers were perturbed by two facts: by clearly perceiving on the one hand that what might rightly be called "classical education" was now only a far-off ideal, a castle in the air, which could not possibly be built as a reality on the foundations of our present educational system, and that, on the other hand, what was now, with customary and unopposed euphemism, pointed to as "classical education" could only claim the value of a pretentious illusion, the best effect of which was that the expression "classical education" still lived on and had not yet lost its pathetic sound. These two worthy men saw clearly, by the system of instruction in vogue, that the time was not yet ripe for a higher culture, a culture founded upon that of the ancients: the neglected state of linguistic instruction; the forcing of students into learned historical paths, instead of giving them a practical training; the connection of certain practices, encouraged in the public schools, with the objectionable spirit of our journalistic publicity—all these easily perceptible phenomena of the teaching of German led to the painful certainty that the most beneficial of those forces which have come down to us from classical antiquity are not yet known in our public schools: forces which would train students for the struggle against the barbarism of the present age, and which will perhaps once more transform the public schools into the arsenals and workshops of this struggle.

On the other hand, it would seem in the meantime as if the spirit of antiquity, in its fundamental principles, had already been driven away from the portals of the public schools, and as if here also the gates were thrown open as widely as possible to the be-flattered and pampered type of our present self-styled "German culture." And if the solitary talkers caught a glimpse of a single ray of hope, it was that things would have to become still worse, that what was as yet divined only by the few would soon be clearly perceived by the many, and that then the time for honest and resolute men for the earnest consideration of the scope of the education of the masses would not be far distant.

After a few minutes' silent reflection, the philosopher's companion turned to him and said: "You used to hold out hopes to me, but now you have done more: you have widened my intelligence, and with it my strength and courage: now indeed can I look on the field of battle with more hardihood, now indeed do I repent of my too hasty flight. We want nothing for ourselves, and it should be nothing to us how many individuals may fall in this battle, or whether we ourselves may be among the first. Just because we take this matter so seriously, we should not take our own poor selves so seriously: at the very moment we are falling some one else will grasp the banner of our faith. I will not even consider whether I am strong enough for such a fight, whether I can offer sufficient resistance; it may even be an honourable death to fall to the accompaniment of the mocking laughter of such enemies, whose seriousness has frequently seemed to us to be something ridiculous. When I think how my contemporaries prepared themselves for the highest posts in the scholastic profession, as I myself have done, then I know how we often laughed at the exact contrary, and grew serious over something quite different——"

"Now, my friend," interrupted the philosopher, laughingly, "you speak as one who would fain dive into the water without being able to swim, and who fears something even more than the mere drowning; *not* being drowned, but laughed at. But being laughed at should be the very last thing for us to dread; for we are in a sphere where there are too many truths to tell, too many formidable, painful, unpardonable truths, for us to escape hatred, and only fury here and there will give rise to some sort of embarrassed laughter. Just think of the innumerable crowd of teachers, who, in all good faith, have assimilated the system of education which has prevailed up to the present, that they may cheerfully and without over-much deliberation carry it further on. What do you think it will seem like to these men when they hear of projects from which they are excluded *beneficio naturæ*; of commands which their mediocre abilities are totally unable to carry out; of hopes which find no echo in them; of battles the war-cries of which they do not understand, and in the fighting of which they can take part only as dull and obtuse rank and file? But, without exaggeration, that must necessarily be the position of practically all the teachers in our higher educational establishments: and indeed we cannot wonder at this when we consider how such a teacher originates, how he *becomes* a teacher of such high status. Such a large number of higher educational establishments are now to be found everywhere that far more teachers will continue to be required for them than the nature of even a highly-gifted people can produce; and thus an inordinate stream of undesirables flows into these institutions, who, however, by their preponderating numbers and their instinct of 'similis simile gaudet' gradually come to determine the nature of these institutions. There may be a few people, hopelessly unfamiliar with pedagogical matters, who believe that our present profusion of public schools and teachers, which is manifestly out of all proportion, can be changed into a real profusion, an *ubertas ingenii*, merely by a few rules and regulations, and without any reduction in the number of these institutions. But we may surely be unanimous in recognising that by the very nature of things only an exceedingly small number of people are destined for a true course of education, and that a much smaller number of higher educational establishments would suffice for their further development, but that, in view of the present large numbers of educational institutions, those for whom in general such institutions ought only to be established must feel themselves to be the least facilitated in their progress.

"The same holds good in regard to teachers. It is precisely the best teachers—those who, generally speaking, judged by a high standard, are worthy of this honourable name—who are now perhaps the least fitted, in view of the present standing of our public schools, for the education of these unselected youths, huddled together in a confused heap; but who must rather, to a certain extent, keep hidden from them the best they could give: and, on the other hand, by far the larger number of these teachers feel themselves quite at home in these institutions, as their moderate abilities stand in a kind of harmonious relationship to the dullness of their pupils. It is from this majority that we hear the ever-resounding call for the establishment of new public schools and higher educational institutions: we are living in an age which, by ringing the changes on its deafening and continual cry, would certainly give one the impression that there was an unprecedented thirst for culture which eagerly sought to be quenched. But it is just at this point that one should learn to hear aright: it is here, without being disconcerted by the thundering noise of the education-mongers, that we must confront those who talk so tirelessly about the educational necessities of their time. Then we should meet with a strange disillusionment, one which we, my good friend, have often met with: those blatant heralds of educational needs, when examined at close quarters, are suddenly seen to be transformed into zealous, yea, fanatical opponents of true culture, *i.e.* all those who hold fast to the aristocratic nature of the mind; for, at bottom, they regard as their goal the emancipation of the masses from the mastery of the great few; they seek to overthrow the most sacred hierarchy in the kingdom of the intellect—the servitude of the masses, their submissive obedience, their instinct of loyalty to the rule of genius.

"I have long accustomed myself to look with caution upon those who are ardent in the cause of the so-called 'education of the people' in the common meaning of the phrase; since for the most part they desire for themselves, consciously or unconsciously, absolutely unlimited freedom, which must inevitably degenerate into something resembling the saturnalia of barbaric times, and which the sacred hierarchy of nature will never grant them. They were born to serve and to obey; and every moment in which their limping or crawling or broken-winded thoughts are at work shows us clearly out of which clay nature moulded them, and what trade mark she branded thereon. The education of the masses cannot, therefore, be our aim; but rather the education of a few picked men for great and lasting works. We well know that a just posterity judges the collective intellectual state of a time only by those few great and lonely figures of the period, and gives its decision in accordance with the manner in which they are recognised, encouraged, and honoured, or, on the other hand, in which they are snubbed, elbowed aside, and kept down. What is called the 'education of the masses' cannot be accomplished except with difficulty; and even if a system of universal compulsory education be applied, they can only be reached outwardly: those individual lower levels where, generally speaking, the masses come into contact with culture, where the people nourishes its religious instinct, where it poetises its mythological images, where it keeps up its faith in its customs, privileges, native soil, and language—all these levels can scarcely be reached by direct means, and in any case only by violent demolition. And, in serious matters of this kind, to hasten forward the progress of the education of the people means simply the postponement of this violent demolition, and the maintenance of that wholesome unconsciousness, that sound sleep, of the people, without which counter-action and remedy no culture, with the exhausting strain and excitement of its own actions, can make any headway.

"We know, however, what the aspiration is of those who would disturb the healthy slumber of the people, and continually call out to them: 'Keep your eyes open! Be sensible! Be wise!' we know the aim of those who profess to satisfy excessive educational requirements by means of an extraordinary increase in the number of educational institutions and the conceited tribe of teachers originated thereby. These very people, using these very means, are fighting against the natural hierarchy in the realm of the intellect, and destroying the roots of all those noble and sublime plastic forces which have their material origin in the unconsciousness of the people, and which fittingly terminate in the procreation of genius and its due guidance and proper training. It is only in the simile of the mother that we can grasp the meaning and the responsibility of the true education of the people in respect to genius: its real origin is not to be found in such education; it has, so to speak, only a metaphysical source, a metaphysical home. But for the genius to make his appearance; for him to emerge from among the people; to portray the reflected picture, as it were, the dazzling brilliancy of the peculiar colours of this people; to depict the noble destiny of a people in the similitude of an individual in a work which will last for all time, thereby making his nation itself eternal, and redeeming it from the ever-shifting element of transient things: all this is possible for the genius only when he has been brought up and come to maturity in the tender care of the culture of a people; whilst, on the other hand, without this sheltering home, the genius will not, generally speaking, be able to rise to the height of his eternal flight, but will at an early moment, like a stranger weather-driven upon a bleak, snow-covered desert, slink away from the inhospitable land."

"You astonish me with such a metaphysics of genius," said the teacher's companion, "and I have only a hazy conception of the accuracy of your similitude. On the other hand, I fully understand what you have said about the surplus of public schools and the corresponding surplus of higher grade teachers; and in this regard I myself have collected some information which assures me that the educational tendency of the public school *must* right itself by this very surplus of teachers who have really nothing at all to do with education, and who are called into existence and pursue this path solely because there is a demand for them. Every man who, in an unexpected moment of enlightenment, has convinced himself of the singularity and inaccessibility of Hellenic antiquity, and has warded off this conviction after an exhausting struggle—every such man knows that the door leading to this enlightenment will never remain open to all comers; and he deems it absurd, yea disgraceful, to use the Greeks as he would any other tool he employs when following his profession or earning his living, shamelessly fumbling with coarse hands amidst the relics of these holy men. This brazen and vulgar feeling is, however, most common in the profession from which the largest numbers of teachers for the public schools are drawn, the philological profession, wherefore the reproduction and continuation of such a feeling in the public school will not surprise us.

"Just look at the younger generation of philologists: how seldom we see in them that humble feeling that we, when compared with such a world as it was, have no right to exist at all: how coolly and fearlessly, as compared with us, did that young brood build its miserable nests in the midst of the magnificent temples! A powerful voice from every nook and cranny should ring in the ears of those who, from the day they begin their connection with the university, roam at will with such self-complacency and shamelessness among the awe-inspiring relics of that noble civilisation: 'Hence, ye uninitiated, who will never be initiated; fly away in silence and shame from these sacred chambers!' But this voice speaks in vain; for one must to some extent be a Greek to understand a Greek curse of excommunication. But these people I am speaking of are so barbaric that they dispose of these relics to suit themselves: all their modern conveniences and fancies are brought with them and concealed among those ancient pillars and tombstones, and it gives rise to great rejoicing when somebody finds, among the dust and cobwebs of antiquity, something that he himself had slyly hidden there not so very long before. One of them makes verses and takes care to consult Hesychius' Lexicon. Something there immediately assures him that he is destined to be an imitator of Æschylus, and leads him to believe, indeed, that he 'has something in common with' Æschylus: the miserable poetaster! Yet another peers with the suspicious eye of a policeman into every contradiction, even into the shadow of every contradiction, of which Homer was guilty: he fritters away his life in tearing Homeric rags to tatters and sewing them together again, rags that he himself was the first to filch from the poet's kingly robe. A third feels ill at ease when examining all the mysterious and orgiastic sides of antiquity: he makes up his mind once and for all to let the enlightened Apollo alone pass without dispute, and to see in the Athenian a gay and intelligent but nevertheless somewhat immoral Apollonian. What a deep breath he draws when he succeeds in raising yet another dark corner of antiquity to the level of his own intelligence!—when, for example, he discovers in Pythagoras a colleague who is as enthusiastic as himself in arguing about politics. Another racks his brains as to why Œdipus was condemned by fate to perform such abominable deeds—killing his father, marrying his mother. Where lies the blame! Where the poetic justice! Suddenly it occurs to him: Œdipus was a passionate fellow, lacking all Christian gentleness—he even fell into an unbecoming rage when Tiresias called him a monster and the curse of the whole country. Be humble and meek! was what Sophocles tried to teach, otherwise you will have to marry your mothers and kill your fathers! Others, again, pass their lives in counting the number of verses written by Greek and Roman poets, and are delighted with the proportions 7:13 = 14:26. Finally, one of them brings forward his solution of a question, such as the Homeric poems considered from the standpoint of prepositions, and thinks he has drawn the truth from the bottom of the well with ἀνά and κατά. All of them, however, with the most widely separated aims in view, dig and burrow in Greek soil with a restlessness and a blundering awkwardness that must surely be painful to a true friend of antiquity: and thus it comes to pass that I should like to take by the hand every talented or talentless man who feels a certain professional inclination urging him on to the study of antiquity, and harangue him as follows: 'Young sir, do you know what perils threaten you, with your little stock of school learning, before you become a man in the full sense of the word? Have you heard that, according to Aristotle, it is by no means a tragic death to be slain by a statue? Does that surprise you? Know, then, that for centuries philologists have been trying, with ever-failing strength, to re-erect the fallen statue of Greek antiquity, but without success; for it is a colossus around which single individual men crawl like pygmies. The leverage of the united representatives of modern culture is utilised for the purpose; but it invariably happens that the huge column is scarcely more than lifted from the ground when it falls down again, crushing beneath its weight the luckless wights under it. That, however, may be tolerated, for every being must perish by some means or other; but who is there to guarantee that during all these attempts the statue itself will not break in pieces! The philologists are being crushed by the Greeks—perhaps we can put up with this—but antiquity itself threatens to be crushed by these philologists! Think that over, you easy-going young man; and turn back, lest you too should not be an iconoclast!'"

"Indeed," said the philosopher, laughing, "there are many philologists who have turned back as you so much desire, and I notice a great contrast with my own youthful experience. Consciously or unconsciously, large numbers of them have concluded that it is hopeless and useless for them to come into direct contact with classical antiquity, hence they are inclined to look upon this study as barren, superseded, out-of-date. This herd has turned with much greater zest to the science of language: here in this wide expanse of virgin soil, where even the most mediocre gifts can be turned to account, and where a kind of insipidity and dullness is even looked upon as decided talent, with the novelty and uncertainty of methods and the constant danger of making fantastic mistakes—here, where dull regimental routine and discipline are desiderata—here the newcomer is no longer frightened by the majestic and warning voice that rises from the ruins of antiquity: here every one is welcomed with open arms, including even him who never arrived at any uncommon impression or noteworthy thought after a perusal of Sophocles and Aristophanes, with the result that they end in an etymological tangle, or are seduced into collecting the fragments of out-of-the-way dialects—and their time is spent in associating and dissociating, collecting and scattering, and running hither and thither consulting books. And such a usefully employed philologist would now fain be a teacher! He now undertakes to teach the youth of the public schools something about the ancient writers, although he himself has read them without any particular impression, much less with insight! What a dilemma! Antiquity has said nothing to him, consequently he has nothing to say about antiquity. A sudden thought strikes him: why is he a skilled philologist at all! Why did these authors write Latin and Greek! And with a light heart he immediately begins to etymologise with Homer, calling Lithuanian or Ecclesiastical Slavonic, or, above all, the sacred Sanskrit, to his assistance: as if Greek lessons were merely the excuse for a general introduction to the study of languages, and as if Homer were lacking in only one respect, namely, not being written in pre-Indogermanic. Whoever is acquainted with our present public schools well knows what a wide gulf separates their teachers from classicism, and how, from a feeling of this want, comparative philology and allied professions have increased their numbers to such an unheard-of degree."

"What I mean is," said the other, "it would depend upon whether a teacher of classical culture did *not* confuse his Greeks and Romans with the other peoples, the barbarians, whether he could *never* put Greek and Latin *on a level with* other languages: so far as his classicalism is concerned, it is a matter of indifference whether the framework of these languages concurs with or is in any way related to the other languages: such a concurrence does not interest him at all; his real concern is with *what is not common to both*, with what shows him that those two peoples were not barbarians as compared with the others—in so far, of course, as he is a true teacher of culture and models himself after the majestic patterns of the classics."

"I may be wrong," said the philosopher, "but I suspect that, owing to the way in which Latin and Greek are now taught in schools, the accurate grasp of these languages, the ability to speak and write them with ease, is lost, and that is something in which my own generation distinguished itself—a generation, indeed, whose few survivers have by this time grown old; whilst, on the other hand, the present teachers seem to impress their pupils with the genetic and historical importance of the subject to such an extent that, at best, their scholars ultimately turn into little Sanskritists, etymological spitfires, or reckless conjecturers; but not one of them can read his Plato or Tacitus with pleasure, as we old folk can. The public schools may still be seats of learning: not, however of *the* learning which, as it were, is only the natural and involuntary auxiliary of a culture that is directed towards the noblest ends; but rather of that culture which might be compared to the hypertrophical swelling of an unhealthy body. The public schools are certainly the seats of this obesity, if, indeed, they have not degenerated into the abodes of that elegant barbarism which is boasted of as being 'German culture of the present!'"

"But," asked the other, "what is to become of that large body of teachers who have not been endowed with a true gift for culture, and who set up as teachers merely to gain a livelihood from the profession, because there is a demand for them, because a superfluity of schools brings with it a superfluity of teachers? Where shall they go when antiquity peremptorily orders them to withdraw? Must they not be sacrificed to those powers of the present who, day after day, call out to them from the never-ending columns of the press: 'We are culture! We are education! We are at the zenith! We are the apexes of the pyramids! We are the aims of universal history!'—when they hear the seductive promises, when the shameful signs of non-culture, the plebeian publicity of the so-called 'interests of culture' are extolled for their benefit in magazines and newspapers as an entirely new and the best possible, full-grown form of culture! Whither shall the poor fellows fly when they feel the presentiment that these promises are not true—where but to the most obtuse, sterile scientificality, that here the shriek of culture may no longer be audible to them? Pursued in this way, must they not end, like the ostrich, by burying their heads in the sand? Is it not a real happiness for them, buried as they are among dialects, etymologies, and conjectures, to lead a life like that of the ants, even though they are miles removed from true culture, if only they can close their ears tightly and be deaf to the voice of the 'elegant' culture of the time."

"You are right, my friend," said the philosopher, "but whence comes the urgent necessity for a surplus of schools for culture, which further gives rise to the necessity for a surplus of teachers?—when we so clearly see that the demand for a surplus springs from a sphere which is hostile to culture, and that the consequences of this surplus only lead to non-culture. Indeed, we can discuss this dire necessity only in so far as the modern State is willing to discuss these things with us, and is prepared to follow up its demands by force: which phenomenon certainly makes the same impression upon most people as if they were addressed by the eternal law of things. For the rest, a 'Culture-State,' to use the current expression, which makes such demands, is rather a novelty, and has only come to a 'self-understanding' within the last half century, *i.e.* in a period when (to use the favourite popular word) so many 'self-understood' things came into being, but which are in themselves not 'self-understood' at all. This right to higher education has been taken so seriously by the most powerful of modern States—Prussia—that the objectionable principle it has adopted, taken in connection with the well-known daring and hardihood of this State, is seen to have a menacing and dangerous consequence for the true German spirit; for we see endeavours being made in this quarter to raise the public school, formally systematised, up to the so-called 'level of the time.' Here is to be found all that mechanism by means of which as many scholars as possible are urged on to take up courses of public school training: here, indeed, the State has its most powerful inducement—the concession of certain privileges respecting military service, with the natural consequence that, according to the unprejudiced evidence of statistical officials, by this, and by this only, can we explain the universal congestion of all Prussian public schools, and the urgent and continual need for new ones. What more can the State do for a surplus of educational institutions than bring all the higher and the majority of the lower civil service appointments, the right of entry to the universities, and even the most influential military posts into close connection with the public school: and all this in a country where both universal military service and the highest offices of the State unconsciously attract all gifted natures to them. The public school is here looked upon as an honourable aim, and every one who feels himself urged on to the sphere of government will be found on his way to it. This is a new and quite original occurrence: the State assumes the attitude of a mystogogue of culture, and, whilst it promotes its own ends, it obliges every one of its servants not to appear in its presence without the torch of universal State education in their hands, by the flickering light of which they may again recognise the State as the highest goal, as the reward of all their strivings after education.

"Now this last phenomenon should indeed surprise them; it should remind them of that allied, slowly understood tendency of a philosophy which was formerly promoted for reasons of State, namely, the tendency of the Hegelian philosophy: yea, it would perhaps be no exaggeration to say that, in the subordination of all strivings after education to reasons of State, Prussia has appropriated, with success, the principle and the useful heirloom of the Hegelian philosophy, whose apotheosis of the State in *this* subordination certainly reaches its height."

"But," said the philosopher's companion, "what purposes can the State have in view with such a strange aim? For that it has some State objects in view is seen in the manner in which the conditions of Prussian schools are admired by, meditated upon, and occasionally imitated by other States. These other States obviously presuppose something here that, if adopted, would tend towards the maintenance and power of the State, like our well-known and popular conscription. Where everyone proudly wears his soldier's uniform at regular intervals, where almost every one has absorbed a uniform type of national culture through the public schools, enthusiastic hyperboles may well be uttered concerning the systems employed in former times, and a form of State omnipotence which was attained only in antiquity, and which almost every young man, by both instinct and training, thinks it is the crowning glory and highest aim of human beings to reach."

"Such a comparison," said the philosopher, "would be quite hyperbolical, and would not hobble along on one leg only. For, indeed, the ancient State emphatically did not share the utilitarian point of view of recognising as culture only what was directly useful to the State itself, and was far from wishing to destroy those impulses which did not seem to be immediately applicable. For this very reason the profound Greek had for the State that strong feeling of admiration and thankfulness which is so distasteful to modern men; because he clearly recognised not only that without such State protection the germs of his culture could not develop, but also that all his inimitable and perennial culture had flourished so luxuriantly under the wise and careful guardianship of the protection afforded by the State. The State was for his culture not a supervisor, regulator, and watchman, but a vigorous and muscular companion and friend, ready for war, who accompanied his noble, admired, and, as it were, ethereal friend through disagreeable reality, earning his thanks therefor. This, however, does not happen when a modern State lays claim to such hearty gratitude because it renders such chivalrous service to German culture and art: for in this regard its past is as ignominious as its present, as a proof of which we have but to think of the manner in which the memory of our great poets and artists is celebrated in German cities, and how the highest objects of these German masters are supported on the part of the State.

"There must therefore be peculiar circumstances surrounding both this purpose towards which the State is tending, and which always promotes what is here called 'education'; and surrounding likewise the culture thus promoted, which subordinates itself to this purpose of the State. With the real German spirit and the education derived therefrom, such as I have slowly outlined for you, this purpose of the State is at war, hiddenly or openly: *the* spirit of education, which is welcomed and encouraged with such interest by the State, and owing to which the schools of this country are so much admired abroad, must accordingly originate in a sphere that never comes into contact with this true German spirit: with that spirit which speaks to us so wondrously from the inner heart of the German Reformation, German music, and German philosophy, and which, like a noble exile, is regarded with such indifference and scorn by the luxurious education afforded by the State. This spirit is a stranger: it passes by in solitary sadness, and far away from it the censer of pseudo-culture is swung backwards and forwards, which, amidst the acclamations of 'educated' teachers and journalists, arrogates to itself its name and privileges, and metes out insulting treatment to the word 'German.' Why does the State require that surplus of educational institutions, of teachers? Why this education of the masses on such an extended scale? Because the true German spirit is hated, because the aristocratic nature of true culture is feared, because the people endeavour in this way to drive single great individuals into self-exile, so that the claims of the masses to education may be, so to speak, planted down and carefully tended, in order that the many may in this way endeavour to escape the rigid and strict discipline of the few great leaders, so that the masses may be persuaded that they can easily find the path for themselves—following the guiding star of the State!

"A new phenomenon! The State as the guiding star of culture! In the meantime one thing consoles me: this German spirit, which people are combating so much, and for which they have substituted a gaudily attired *locum tenens*, this spirit is brave: it will fight and redeem itself into a purer age; noble, as it is now, and victorious, as it one day will be, it will always preserve in its mind a certain pitiful toleration of the State, if the latter, hard-pressed in the hour of extremity, secures such a pseudo-culture as its associate. For what, after all, do we know about the difficult task of governing men, *i.e.* to keep law, order, quietness, and peace among millions of boundlessly egoistical, unjust, unreasonable, dishonourable, envious, malignant, and hence very narrow-minded and perverse human beings; and thus to protect the few things that the State has conquered for itself against covetous neighbours and jealous robbers? Such a hard-pressed State holds out its arms to any associate, grasps at any straw; and when such an associate does introduce himself with flowery eloquence, when he adjudges the State, as Hegel did, to be an 'absolutely complete ethical organism,' the be-all and end-all of every one's education, and goes on to indicate how he himself can best promote the interests of the State—who will be surprised if, without further parley, the State falls upon his neck and cries aloud in a barbaric voice of full conviction: 'Yes! Thou art education! Thou art indeed culture!'"

Fourth Lecture.

(Delivered on the 5th of March 1872.)

Ladies and Gentlemen,—Now that you have followed my tale up to this point, and that we have made ourselves joint masters of the solitary, remote, and at times abusive duologue of the philosopher and his companion, I sincerely hope that you, like strong swimmers, are ready to proceed on the second half of our journey, especially as I can promise you that a few other marionettes will appear in the puppet-play of my adventure, and that if up to the present you have only been able to do little more than endure what I have been telling you, the waves of my story will now bear you more quickly and easily towards the end. In other words we have now come to a turning, and it would be advisable for us to take a short glance backwards to see what we think we have gained from such a varied conversation.

"Remain in your present position," the philosopher seemed to say to his companion, "for you may cherish hopes. It is more and more clearly evident that we have no educational institutions at all; but that we ought to have them. Our public schools—established, it would seem, for this high object—have either become the nurseries of a reprehensible culture which repels the true culture with profound hatred—*i.e.* a true, aristocratic culture, founded upon a few carefully chosen minds; or they foster a micrological and sterile learning which, while it is far removed from culture, has at least this merit, that it avoids that reprehensible culture as well as the true culture." The philosopher had particularly drawn his companion's attention to the strange corruption which must have entered into the heart of culture when the State thought itself capable of tyrannising over it and of attaining its ends through it; and further when the State, in conjunction with this culture, struggled against other hostile forces as well as against *the* spirit which the philosopher ventured to call the "true German spirit." This spirit, linked to the Greeks by the noblest ties, and shown by its past history to have been steadfast and courageous, pure and lofty in its aims, its faculties qualifying it for the high task of freeing modern man from the curse of modernity—this spirit is condemned to live apart, banished from its inheritance. But when its slow, painful tones of woe resound through the desert of the present, then the overladen and gaily-decked caravan of culture is pulled up short, horror-stricken. We must not only astonish, but terrify—such was the philosopher's opinion: not to fly shamefully away, but to take the offensive, was his advice; but he especially counselled his companion not to ponder too anxiously over the individual from whom, through a higher instinct, this aversion for the present barbarism proceeded, "Let it perish: the Pythian god had no difficulty in finding a new tripod, a second Pythia, so long, at least, as the mystic cold vapours rose from the earth."

The philosopher once more began to speak: "Be careful to remember, my friend," said he, "there are two things you must not confuse. A man must learn a great deal that he may live and take part in the struggle for existence; but everything that he as an individual learns and does with this end in view has nothing whatever to do with culture. This latter only takes its beginning in a sphere that lies far above the world of necessity, indigence, and struggle for existence. The question now is to what extent a man values his ego in comparison with other egos, how much of his strength he uses up in the endeavour to earn his living. Many a one, by stoically confining his needs within a narrow compass, will shortly and easily reach the sphere in which he may forget, and, as it were, shake off his ego, so that he can enjoy perpetual youth in a solar system of timeless and impersonal things. Another widens the scope and needs of his ego as much as possible, and builds the mausoleum of this ego in vast proportions, as if he were prepared to fight and conquer that terrible adversary, Time. In this instinct also we may see a longing for immortality: wealth and power, wisdom, presence of mind, eloquence, a flourishing outward aspect, a renowned name—all these are merely turned into the means by which an insatiable, personal will to live craves for new life, with which, again, it hankers after an eternity that is at last seen to be illusory.

"But even in this highest form of the ego, in the enhanced needs of such a distended and, as it were, collective individual, true culture is never touched upon; and if, for example, art is sought after, only its disseminating and stimulating actions come into prominence, *i.e.* those which least give rise to pure and noble art, and most of all to low and degraded forms of it. For in all his efforts, however great and exceptional they seem to the onlooker, he never succeeds in freeing himself from his own hankering and restless personality: that illuminated, ethereal sphere where one may contemplate without the obstruction of one's own personality continually recedes from him—and thus, let him learn, travel, and collect as he may, he must always live an exiled life at a remote distance from a higher life and from true culture. For true culture would scorn to contaminate itself with the needy and covetous individual; it well knows how to give the slip to the man who would fain employ it as a means of attaining to egoistic ends; and if any one cherishes the belief that he has firmly secured it as a means of livelihood, and that he can procure the necessities of life by its sedulous cultivation, then it suddenly steals away with noiseless steps and an air of derisive mockery.[6]

"I will thus ask you, my friend, not to confound this culture, this sensitive, fastidious, ethereal goddess, with that useful maid-of-all-work which is also called 'culture,' but which is only the intellectual servant and counsellor of one's practical necessities, wants, and means of livelihood. Every kind of training, however, which holds out the prospect of bread-winning as its end and aim, is not a training for culture as we understand the word; but merely a collection of precepts and directions to show how, in the struggle for existence, a man may preserve and protect his own person. It may be freely admitted that for the great majority of men such a course of instruction is of the highest importance; and the more arduous the struggle is the more intensely must the young man strain every nerve to utilise his strength to the best advantage.

"But—let no one think for a moment that the schools which urge him on to this struggle and prepare him for it are in any way seriously to be considered as establishments of culture. They are institutions which teach one how to take part in the battle of life; whether they promise to turn out civil servants, or merchants, or officers, or wholesale dealers, or farmers, or physicians, or men with a technical training. The regulations and standards prevailing at such institutions differ from those in a true educational institution; and what in the latter is permitted, and even freely held out as often as possible, ought to be considered as a criminal offence in the former.

[6] It will be apparent from these words that Nietzsche is still under the influence of Schopenhauer.—Tr.

"Let me give you an example. If you wish to guide a young man on the path of true culture, beware of interrupting his naive, confident, and, as it were, immediate and personal relationship with nature. The woods, the rocks, the winds, the vulture, the flowers, the butterfly, the meads, the mountain slopes, must all speak to him in their own language; in them he must, as it were, come to know himself again in countless reflections and images, in a variegated round of changing visions; and in this way he will unconsciously and gradually feel the metaphysical unity of all things in the great image of nature, and at the same time tranquillise his soul in the contemplation of her eternal endurance and necessity. But how many young men should be permitted to grow up in such close and almost personal proximity to nature! The others must learn another truth betimes: how to subdue nature to themselves. Here is an end of this naive metaphysics; and the physiology of plants and animals, geology, inorganic chemistry, force their devotees to view nature from an altogether different standpoint. What is lost by this new point of view is not only a poetical phantasmagoria, but the instinctive, true, and unique point of view, instead of which we have shrewd and clever calculations, and, so to speak, overreachings of nature. Thus to the truly cultured man is vouchsafed the inestimable benefit of being able to remain faithful, without a break, to the contemplative instincts of his childhood, and so to attain to a calmness, unity, consistency, and harmony which can never be even thought of by a man who is compelled to fight in the struggle for existence.

"You must not think, however, that I wish to withhold all praise from our primary and secondary schools: I honour the seminaries where boys learn arithmetic and master modern languages, and study geography and the marvellous discoveries made in natural science. I am quite prepared to say further that those youths who pass through the better class of secondary schools are well entitled to make the claims put forward by the fully-fledged public school boy; and the time is certainly not far distant when such pupils will be everywhere freely admitted to the universities and positions under the government, which has hitherto been the case only with scholars from the public schools—of our present public schools, be it noted![7] I cannot, however, refrain from adding the melancholy reflection: if it be true that secondary and public schools are, on the whole, working so heartily in common towards the same ends, and differ from each other only in such a slight degree, that they may take equal rank before the tribunal of the State,

[7] This prophecy has come true.—Tr.

then we completely lack another kind of educational institutions: those for the development of culture! To say the least, the secondary schools cannot be reproached with this; for they have up to the present propitiously and honourably followed up tendencies of a lower order, but one nevertheless highly necessary. In the public schools, however, there is very much less honesty and very much less ability too; for in them we find an instinctive feeling of shame, the unconscious perception of the fact that the whole institution has been ignominiously degraded, and that the sonorous words of wise and apathetic teachers are contradictory to the dreary, barbaric, and sterile reality. So there are no true cultural institutions! And in those very places where a pretence to culture is still kept up, we find the people more hopeless, atrophied, and discontented than in the secondary schools, where the so-called 'realistic' subjects are taught! Besides this, only think how immature and uninformed one must be in the company of such teachers when one actually misunderstands the rigorously defined philosophical expressions 'real' and 'realism' to such a degree as to think them the contraries of mind and matter, and to interpret 'realism' as 'the road to knowledge, formation, and mastery of reality.'

"I for my own part know of only two exact contraries: *institutions for teaching culture and institutions for teaching how to succeed in life*. All our present institutions belong to the second class; but I am speaking only of the first."

About two hours went by while the philosophically-minded couple chatted about such startling questions. Night slowly fell in the meantime; and when in the twilight the philosopher's voice had sounded like natural music through the woods, it now rang out in the profound darkness of the night when he was speaking with excitement or even passionately; his tones hissing and thundering far down the valley, and reverberating among the trees and rocks. Suddenly he was silent: he had just repeated, almost pathetically, the words, "we have no true educational institutions; we have no true educational institutions!" when something fell down just in front of him—it might have been a fir-cone—and his dog barked and ran towards it. Thus interrupted, the philosopher raised his head, and suddenly became aware of the darkness, the cool air, and the lonely situation of himself and his companion. "Well! What are we about!" he ejaculated, "it's dark. You know whom we were expecting here; but he hasn't come. We have waited in vain; let us go."

I must now, ladies and gentlemen, convey to you the impressions experienced by my friend and myself as we eagerly listened to this conversation, which we heard distinctly in our hiding-place. I have already told you that at that place and at that hour we had intended to hold a festival in commemoration of something: and this something had to do with nothing else than matters concerning educational training, of which we, in our own youthful opinions, had garnered a plentiful harvest during our past life. We were thus disposed to remember with gratitude the institution which we had at one time thought out for ourselves at that very spot in order, as I have already mentioned, that we might reciprocally encourage and watch over one another's educational impulses. But a sudden and unexpected light was thrown on all that past life as we silently gave ourselves up to the vehement words of the philosopher. As when a traveller, walking heedlessly across unknown ground, suddenly puts his foot over the edge of a cliff, so it now seemed to us that we had hastened to meet the great danger rather than run away from it. Here at this spot, so memorable to us, we heard the warning: "Back! Not another step! Know you not whither your footsteps tend, whither this deceitful path is luring you?"

It seemed to us that we now knew, and our feeling of overflowing thankfulness impelled us so irresistibly towards our earnest counsellor and trusty Eckart, that both of us sprang up at the same moment and rushed towards the philosopher to embrace him. He was just about to move off, and had already turned sideways when we rushed up to him. The dog turned sharply round and barked, thinking doubtless, like the philosopher's companion, of an attempt at robbery rather than an enraptured embrace. It was plain that he had forgotten us. In a word, he ran away. Our embrace was a miserable failure when we did overtake him; for my friend gave a loud yell as the dog bit him, and the philosopher himself sprang away from me with such force that we both fell. What with the dog and the men there was a scramble that lasted a few minutes, until my friend began to call out loudly, parodying the philosopher's own words: "In the name of all culture and pseudo-culture, what does the silly dog want with us? Hence, you confounded dog; you uninitiated, never to be initiated; hasten away from us, silent and ashamed!" After this outburst matters were cleared up to some extent, at any rate so far as they could be cleared up in the darkness of the wood. "Oh, it's you!" ejaculated the philosopher, "our duellists! How you startled us! What on earth drives you to jump out upon us like this at such a time of the night?"

“Joy, thankfulness, and reverence,” said we, shaking the old man by the hand, whilst the dog barked as if he understood, “we can’t let you go without telling you this. And if you are to understand everything you must not go away just yet; we want to ask you about so many things that lie heavily on our hearts. Stay yet awhile; we know every foot of the way and can accompany you afterwards. The gentleman you expect may yet turn up. Look over yonder on the Rhine: what is that we see so clearly floating on the surface of the water as if surrounded by the light of many torches? It is there that we may look for your friend, I would even venture to say that it is he who is coming towards you with all those lights.”

And so much did we assail the surprised old man with our entreaties, promises, and fantastic delusions, that we persuaded the philosopher to walk to and fro with us on the little plateau, “by learned lumber undisturbed,” as my friend added.

“Shame on you!” said the philosopher, “if you really want to quote something, why choose Faust? However, I will give in to you, quotation or no quotation, if only our young companions will keep still and not run away as suddenly as they made their appearance, for they are like will-o’-the-wisps; we are amazed when they are there and again when they are not there.”

My friend immediately recited—

Respect, I hope, will teach us how we may
Our lighter disposition keep at bay.
Our course is only zig-zag as a rule.

The philosopher was surprised, and stood still. “You astonish me, you will-o’-the-wisps,” he said; “this is no quagmire we are on now. Of what use is this ground to you? What does the proximity of a philosopher mean to you? For around him the air is sharp and clear, the ground dry and hard. You must find out a more fantastic region for your zig-zagging inclinations.”

“I think,” interrupted the philosopher’s companion at this point, “the gentlemen have already told us that they promised to meet some one here at this hour; but it seems to me that they listened to our comedy of education like a chorus, and truly ‘idealistic spectators’—for they did not disturb us; we thought we were alone with each other.”

"Yes, that is true," said the philosopher, "that praise must not be withheld from them, but it seems to me that they deserve still higher praise——"

Here I seized the philosopher's hand and said: "That man must be as obtuse as a reptile, with his stomach on the ground and his head buried in mud, who can listen to such a discourse as yours without becoming earnest and thoughtful, or even excited and indignant. Self-accusation and annoyance might perhaps cause a few to get angry; but our impression was quite different: the only thing I do not know is how exactly to describe it. This hour was so well-timed for us, and our minds were so well prepared, that we sat there like empty vessels, and now it seems as if we were filled to overflowing with this new wisdom: for I no longer know how to help myself, and if some one asked me what I am thinking of doing to-morrow, or what I have made up my mind to do with myself from now on, I should not know what to answer. For it is easy to see that we have up to the present been living and educating ourselves in the wrong way—but what can we do to cross over the chasm between to-day and to-morrow?"

"Yes," acknowledged my friend, "I have a similar feeling, and I ask the same question: but besides that I feel as if I were frightened away from German culture by entertaining such high and ideal views of its task; yea, as if I were unworthy to co-operate with it in carrying out its aims. I only see a resplendent file of the highest natures moving towards this goal; I can imagine over what abysses and through what temptations this procession travels. Who would dare to be so bold as to join in it?"

At this point the philosopher's companion again turned to him and said: "Don't be angry with me when I tell you that I too have a somewhat similar feeling, which I have not mentioned to you before. When talking to you I often felt drawn out of myself, as it were, and inspired with your ardour and hopes till I almost forgot myself. Then a calmer moment arrives; a piercing wind of reality brings me back to earth—and then I see the wide gulf between us, over which you yourself, as in a dream, draw me back again. Then what you call 'culture' merely totters meaninglessly around me or lies heavily on my breast: it is like a shirt of mail that weighs me down, or a sword that I cannot wield."

Our minds, as we thus argued with the philosopher, were unanimous, and, mutually encouraging and stimulating one another, we slowly walked with him backwards and forwards along the unencumbered space which had earlier in the day served us as a shooting range. And then, in the still night, under the peaceful light of hundreds of stars, we all broke out into a tirade which ran somewhat as follows:—

"You have told us so much about the genius," we began, "about his lonely and wearisome journey through the world, as if nature never exhibited anything but the most diametrical contraries: in one place the stupid, dull masses, acting by instinct, and then, on a far higher and more remote plane, the great contemplating few, destined for the production of immortal works. But now you call these the apexes of the intellectual pyramid: it would, however, seem that between the broad, heavily burdened foundation up to the highest of the free and unencumbered peaks there must be countless intermediate degrees, and that here we must apply the saying *natura non facit saltus*. Where then are we to look for the beginning of what you call culture; where is the line of demarcation to be drawn between the spheres which are ruled from below upwards and those which are ruled from above downwards? And if it be only in connection with these exalted beings that true culture may be spoken of, how are institutions to be founded for the uncertain existence of such natures, how can we devise educational establishments which shall be of benefit only to these select few? It rather seems to us that such persons know how to find their own way, and that their full strength is shown in their being able to walk without the educational crutches necessary for other people, and thus undisturbed to make their way through the storm and stress of this rough world just like a phantom."

We kept on arguing in this fashion, speaking without any great ability and not putting our thoughts in any special form: but the philosopher's companion went even further, and said to him: "Just think of all these great geniuses of whom we are wont to be so proud, looking upon them as tried and true leaders and guides of this real German spirit, whose names we commemorate by statues and festivals, and whose works we hold up with feelings of pride for the admiration of foreign lands—how did they obtain the education you demand for them, to what degree do they show that they have been nourished and matured by basking in the sun of national education? And yet they are seen to be possible, they have nevertheless become men whom we must honour: yea, their works themselves justify the form of the development of these noble spirits; they justify even a certain want of education for which we must make allowance owing to their country and the age in which they lived. How could Lessing and Winckelmann benefit by the German culture of their time? Even less than, or at all events just as little as Beethoven, Schiller, Goethe, or every one of our great poets and artists. It may perhaps be a law of nature that only the later generations are destined to know by what divine gifts an earlier generation was favoured."

At this point the old philosopher could not control his anger, and shouted to his companion: "Oh, you innocent lamb of knowledge! You gentle sucking doves, all of you! And would you give the name of arguments to those distorted, clumsy, narrow-minded, ungainly, crippled things? Yes, I have just now been listening to the fruits of some of this present-day culture, and my ears are still ringing with the sound of historical 'self-understood' things, of over-wise and pitiless historical reasonings! Mark this, thou unprofaned Nature: thou hast grown old, and for thousands of years this starry sky has spanned the space above thee—but thou hast never yet heard such conceited and, at bottom, mischievous chatter as the talk of the present day! So you are proud of your poets and artists, my good Teutons? You point to them and brag about them to foreign countries, do you? And because it has given you no trouble to have them amongst you, you have formed the pleasant theory that you need not concern yourselves further with them? Isn't that so, my inexperienced children: they come of their own free will, the stork brings them to you! Who would dare to mention a midwife! You deserve an earnest teaching, eh? You should be proud of the fact that all the noble and brilliant men we have mentioned were prematurely suffocated, worn out, and crushed through you, through your barbarism? You think without shame of Lessing, who, on account of your stupidity, perished in battle against your ludicrous gods and idols, the evils of your theatres, your learned men, and your theologians, without once daring to lift himself to the height of that immortal flight for which he was brought into the world. And what are your impressions when you think of Winckelmann, who, that he might rid his eyes of your grotesque fatuousness, went to beg help from the Jesuits, and whose disgraceful religious conversion recoils upon you and will always remain an ineffaceable blemish upon you? You can even name Schiller without blushing! Just look at his picture! The fiery, sparkling eyes, looking at you with disdain, those flushed, death-like cheeks: can you learn nothing from all that? In him you had a beautiful and divine plaything, and through it was destroyed. And if it had been possible for you to take Goethe's friendship away from this melancholy, hasty life, hunted to premature death, then you would have crushed him even sooner than you did. You have not rendered assistance to a single one of our great geniuses—and now upon that fact you wish to build up the theory that none of them shall ever be helped in future? For each of them, however, up to this very moment, you have always been the 'resistance of the stupid world' that Goethe speaks of in his "Epilogue to the Bell"; towards each of them you acted the part of apathetic dullards or jealous narrow-hearts or malignant egotists. In spite of you they created their immortal works, against you they directed their attacks, and thanks to you they died so prematurely, their tasks only half accomplished, blunted and dulled and shattered in the battle. Who can tell to what these heroic men were destined to attain if only that true German spirit had gathered them together within the protecting walls of a powerful institution?—that spirit which, without the help of some such institution, drags out an isolated, debased, and degraded existence. All those great men were utterly ruined; and it is only an insane belief in the Hegelian 'reasonableness of all happenings' which would absolve you of any responsibility in the matter. And not those men alone! Indictments are pouring forth against you from every intellectual province: whether I look at the talents of our poets, philosophers, painters, or sculptors—and not only in the case of gifts of the highest order—I everywhere see immaturity, overstrained nerves, or prematurely exhausted energies, abilities wasted and nipped in the bud; I everywhere feel that 'resistance of the stupid world,' in other words, *your* guiltiness. That is what I am talking about when I speak of lacking educational establishments, and why I think those which at present claim the name in such a pitiful condition. Whoever is pleased to call this an 'ideal desire,' and refers to it as 'ideal' as if he were trying to get rid of it by praising me, deserves the answer that the present system is a scandal and a disgrace, and that the man who asks for warmth in the midst of ice and snow must indeed get angry if he hears this referred to as an 'ideal desire.' The matter we are now discussing is concerned with clear, urgent, and palpably evident realities: a man who knows anything of the question feels that there is a need which must be seen to, just like cold and hunger. But the man who is not affected at all by this matter most certainly has a standard by which to measure the extent of his own culture, and thus to know what I call 'culture,' and where the line should be drawn between that which is ruled from below upwards and that which is ruled from above downwards."

The philosopher seemed to be speaking very heatedly. We begged him to walk round with us again, since he had uttered the latter part of his discourse standing near the tree-stump which had served us as a target. For a few minutes not a word more was spoken. Slowly and thoughtfully we walked to and fro. We did not so much feel ashamed of having brought forward such foolish arguments as we felt a kind of restitution of our personality. After the heated and, so far as we were concerned, very unflattering utterance of the philosopher, we seemed to feel ourselves nearer to him—that we even stood in a personal relationship to him. For so wretched is man that he never feels himself brought into such close contact with a stranger as when the latter shows some sign of weakness, some defect. That our philosopher had lost his temper and made use of abusive language helped to bridge over the gulf created between us by our timid respect for him: and for the sake of the reader who feels his indignation rising at this suggestion let it be added that this bridge often leads from distant hero-worship to personal love and pity. And, after the feeling that our personality had been restored to us, this pity gradually became stronger and stronger. Why were we making this old man walk up and down with us between the rocks and trees at that time of the night? And, since he had yielded to our entreaties, why could we not have thought of a more modest and unassuming manner of having ourselves instructed, why should the three of us have contradicted him in such clumsy terms?

For now we saw how thoughtless, unprepared, and baseless were all the objections we had made, and how greatly the echo of *the* present was heard in them, the voice of which, in the province of culture, the old man would fain not have heard. Our objections, however, were not purely intellectual ones: our reasons for protesting against the philosopher's statements seemed to lie elsewhere. They arose perhaps from the instinctive anxiety to know whether, if the philosopher's views were carried into effect, our own personalities would find a place in the higher or lower division; and this made it necessary for us to find some arguments against the mode of thinking which robbed us of our self-styled claims to culture. People, however, should not argue with companions who feel the weight of an argument so personally; or, as the moral in our case would have been: such companions should not argue, should not contradict at all.

So we walked on beside the philosopher, ashamed, compassionate, dissatisfied with ourselves, and more than ever convinced that the old man was right and that we had done him wrong. How remote now seemed the youthful dream of our educational institution; how clearly we saw the danger which we had hitherto escaped merely by good luck, namely, giving ourselves up body and soul to the educational system which forced itself upon our notice so enticingly, from the time when we entered the public schools up to that moment. How then had it come about that we had not taken our places in the chorus of its admirers? Perhaps merely because we were real students, and could still draw back from the rough-and-tumble, the pushing and struggling, the restless, ever-breaking waves of publicity, to seek refuge in our own little educational establishment; which, however, time would have soon swallowed up also.

Overcome by such reflections, we were about to address the philosopher again, when he suddenly turned towards us, and said in a softer tone—

"I cannot be surprised if you young men behave rashly and thoughtlessly; for it is hardly likely that you have ever seriously considered what I have just said to you. Don't be in a hurry; carry this question about with you, but do at any rate consider it day and night. For you are now at the parting of the ways, and now you know where each path leads. If you take the one, your age will receive you with open arms, you will not find it wanting in honours and decorations: you will form units of an enormous rank and file; and there will be as many people like-minded standing behind you as in front of you. And when the leader gives the word it will be re-echoed from rank to rank. For here your first duty is this: to fight in rank and file; and your second: to annihilate all those who refuse to form part of the rank and file. On the other path you will have but few fellow-travellers: it is more arduous, winding and precipitous; and those who take the first path will mock you, for your progress is more wearisome, and they will try to lure you over into their own ranks. When the two paths happen to cross, however, you will be roughly handled and thrust aside, or else shunned and isolated.

"Now, take these two parties, so different from each other in every respect, and tell me what meaning an educational establishment would have for them. That enormous horde, crowding onwards on the first path towards its goal, would take the term to mean an institution by which each of its members would become duly qualified to take his place in the rank and file, and would be purged of everything which might tend to make him strive after higher and more remote aims. I don't deny, of course, that they can find pompous words with which to describe their aims: for example, they speak of the 'universal development of free personality upon a firm social, national, and human basis,' or they announce as their goal: 'The founding of the peaceful sovereignty of the people upon reason, education, and justice.'

"An educational establishment for the other and smaller company, however, would be something vastly different. They would employ it to prevent themselves from being separated from one another and overwhelmed by the first huge crowd, to prevent their few select spirits from losing sight of their splendid and noble task through premature weariness, or from being turned aside from the true path, corrupted, or subverted. These select spirits must complete their work: that is the *raison d'être* of their common institution—a work, indeed, which, as it were, must be free from subjective traces, and must further rise above the transient events of future times as the pure reflection of the eternal and immutable essence of things. And all those who occupy places in that institution must co-operate in the endeavour to engender men of genius by this purification from subjectiveness and the creation of the works of genius. Not a few, even of those whose talents may be of the second or third order, are suited to such co-operation, and only when serving in such an educational establishment as this do they feel that they are truly carrying out their life's task. But now it is just these talents I speak of which are drawn away from the true path, and their instincts estranged, by the continual seductions of that modern 'culture.'

"The egotistic emotions, weaknesses, and vanities of these few select minds are continually assailed by the temptations unceasingly murmured into their ears by the spirit of the age: 'Come with me! There you are servants, retainers, tools, eclipsed by higher natures; your own peculiar characteristics never have free play; you are tied down, chained down, like slaves; yea, like automata: here, with me, you will enjoy the freedom of your own personalities, as masters should, your talents will cast their lustre on yourselves alone, with their aid you may come to the very front rank; an innumerable train of followers will accompany you, and the applause of public opinion will yield you more pleasure than a nobly-bestowed commendation from the height of genius.' Even the very best of men now yield to these temptations: and it cannot be said that the deciding factor here is the degree of talent, or whether a man is accessible to these voices or not; but rather the degree and the height of a certain moral sublimity, the instinct towards heroism, towards sacrifice—and finally a positive, habitual need of culture, prepared by a proper kind of education, which education, as I have previously said, is first and foremost obedience and submission to the discipline of genius. Of this discipline and submission, however, the present institutions called by courtesy 'educational establishments' know nothing whatever, although I have no doubt that the public school was originally intended to be an institution for sowing the seeds of true culture, or at least as a preparation for it. I have no doubt, either, that they took the first bold steps in the wonderful and stirring times of the Reformation, and that afterwards, in the era which gave birth to Schiller and Goethe, there was again a growing demand for culture, like the first protuberance of that wing spoken of by Plato in the *Phaedrus*, which, at every contact with the beautiful, bears the soul aloft into the upper regions, the habitations of the gods."

"Ah," began the philosopher's companion, "when you quote the divine Plato and the world of ideas, I do not think you are angry with me, however much my previous utterance may have merited your disapproval and wrath. As soon as you speak of it, I feel that Platonic wing rising within me; and it is only at intervals, when I act as the charioteer of my soul, that I have any difficulty with the resisting and unwilling horse that Plato has also described to us, the 'crooked, lumbering animal, put together anyhow, with a short, thick neck; flat-faced, and of a dark colour, with grey eyes and blood-red complexion; the mate of insolence and pride, shag-eared and deaf, hardly yielding to whip or spur.'[8] Just think how long I have lived at a distance from you, and how all those temptations you speak of have endeavoured to lure me away, not perhaps without some success, even though I myself may not have observed it. I now see more clearly than ever the necessity for an institution which will enable us to live and mix freely with the few men of true culture, so that we may have them as our leaders and guiding stars. How greatly I feel the danger of travelling alone! And when it occurred to me that I could save myself by flight from all contact with the spirit of the time, I found that this flight itself was a mere delusion. Continuously, with every breath we take, some amount of that atmosphere circulates through every vein and artery, and no solitude is lonesome or distant enough for us to be out of reach of its fogs and clouds. Whether in the guise of hope, doubt, profit, or virtue, the shades of that culture hover about us; and we have been deceived by that jugglery even here in the presence of a true hermit of culture. How steadfastly and faithfully must the few followers of that culture—which might almost be called sectarian—be ever on the alert! How they must strengthen and uphold one another! How adversely would any errors be criticised here, and how sympathetically excused! And thus, teacher, I ask you to pardon me, after you have laboured so earnestly to set me in the right path!"

[8] *Phaedrus*; Jowett's translation.

"You use a language which I do not care for, my friend," said the philosopher, "and one which reminds me of a diocesan conference. With that I have nothing to do. But your Platonic horse pleases me, and on its account you shall be forgiven. I am willing to exchange my own animal for yours. But it is getting chilly, and I don't feel inclined to walk about any more just now. The friend I was waiting for is indeed foolish enough to come up here even at midnight if he promised to do so. But I have waited in vain for the signal agreed upon; and I cannot guess what has delayed him. For as a rule he is punctual, as we old men are wont, to be, something that you young men nowadays look upon as old-fashioned. But he has left me in the lurch for once: how annoying it is! Come away with me! It's time to go!"

At this moment something happened.

Fifth Lecture.

(Delivered on the 23rd of March 1872.)

Ladies and Gentlemen,—If you have lent a sympathetic ear to what I have told you about the heated argument of our philosopher in the stillness of that memorable night, you must have felt as disappointed as we did when he announced his peevish intention. You will remember that he had suddenly told us he wished to go; for, having been left in the lurch by his friend in the first place, and, in the second, having been bored rather than animated by the remarks addressed to him by his companion and ourselves when walking backwards and forwards on the hillside, he now apparently wanted to put an end to what appeared to him to be a useless discussion. It must have seemed to him that his day had been lost, and he would have liked to blot it out of his memory, together with the recollection of ever having made our acquaintance. And we were thus rather unwillingly preparing to depart when something else suddenly brought him to a standstill, and the foot he had just raised sank hesitatingly to the ground again.

A coloured flame, making a crackling noise for a few seconds, attracted our attention from the direction of the Rhine; and immediately following upon this we heard a slow, harmonious call, quite in tune, although plainly the cry of numerous youthful voices. "That's his signal," exclaimed the philosopher, "so my friend is really coming, and I haven't waited for nothing, after all. It will be a midnight meeting indeed—but how am I to let him know that I am still here? Come! Your pistols; let us see your talent once again! Did you hear the severe rhythm of that melody saluting us? Mark it well, and answer it in the same rhythm by a series of shots."

This was a task well suited to our tastes and abilities; so we loaded up as quickly as we could and pointed our weapons at the brilliant stars in the heavens, whilst the echo of that piercing cry died away in the distance. The reports of the first, second, and third shots sounded sharply in the stillness; and then the philosopher cried "False time!" as our rhythm was suddenly interrupted: for, like a lightning flash, a shooting star tore its way across the clouds after the third report, and almost involuntarily our fourth and fifth shots were sent after it in the direction it had taken.

"False time!" said the philosopher again, "who told you to shoot stars! They can fall well enough without you! People should know what they want before they begin to handle weapons."

And then we once more heard that loud melody from the waters of the Rhine, intoned by numerous and strong voices. "They understand us," said the philosopher, laughing, "and who indeed could resist when such a dazzling phantom comes within range?" "Hush!" interrupted his friend, "what sort of a company can it be that returns the signal to us in such a way? I should say they were between twenty and forty strong, manly voices in that crowd—and where would such a number come from to greet us? They don't appear to have left the opposite bank of the Rhine yet; but at any rate we must have a look at them from our own side of the river. Come along, quickly!"

We were then standing near the top of the hill, you may remember, and our view of the river was interrupted by a dark, thick wood. On the other hand, as I have told you, from the quiet little spot which we had left we could have a better view than from the little plateau on the hillside; and the Rhine, with the island of Nonnenwörth in the middle, was just visible to the beholder who peered over the tree-tops. We therefore set off hastily towards this little spot, taking care, however, not to go too quickly for the philosopher's comfort. The night was pitch dark, and we seemed to find our way by instinct rather than by clearly distinguishing the path, as we walked down with the philosopher in the middle.

We had scarcely reached our side of the river when a broad and fiery, yet dull and uncertain light shot up, which plainly came from the opposite side of the Rhine. "Those are torches," I cried, "there is nothing surer than that my comrades from Bonn are over yonder, and that your friend must be with them. It is they who sang that peculiar song, and they have doubtless accompanied your friend here. See! Listen! They are putting off in little boats. The whole torchlight procession will have arrived here in less than half an hour."

The philosopher jumped back. "What do you say?" he ejaculated, "your comrades from Bonn—students—can my friend have come here with *students*?"

This question, uttered almost wrathfully, provoked us. "What's your objection to students?" we demanded; but there was no answer. It was only after a pause that the philosopher slowly began to speak, not addressing us directly, as it were, but rather some one in the distance: "So, my friend, even at midnight, even on the top of a lonely mountain, we shall not be alone; and you yourself are bringing a pack of mischief-making students along with you, although you well know that I am only too glad to get out of the way of *hoc genus omne*. I don't quite understand you, my friend: it must mean something when we arrange to meet after a long separation at such an out-of-the-way place and at such an unusual hour. Why should we want a crowd of witnesses—and such witnesses! What calls us together to-day is least of all a sentimental, soft-hearted necessity; for both of us learnt early in life to live alone in dignified isolation. It was not for our own sakes, not to show our tender feelings towards each other, or to perform an unrehearsed act of friendship, that we decided to meet here; but that here, where I once came suddenly upon you as you sat in majestic solitude, we might earnestly deliberate with each other like knights of a new order. Let them listen to us who can understand us; but why should you bring with you a throng of people who don't understand us! I don't know what you mean by such a thing, my friend!"

We did not think it proper to interrupt the dissatisfied old grumbler; and as he came to a melancholy close we did not dare to tell him how greatly this distrustful repudiation of students vexed us.

At last the philosopher's companion turned to him and said: "I am reminded of the fact that even you at one time, before I made your acquaintance, occupied posts in several universities, and that reports concerning your intercourse with the students and your methods of instruction at the time are still in circulation. From the tone of resignation in which you have just referred to students many would be inclined to think that you had some peculiar experiences which were not at all to your liking; but personally I rather believe that you saw and experienced in such places just what every one else saw and experienced in them, but that you judged what you saw and felt more justly and severely than any one else. For, during the time I have known you, I have learnt that the most noteworthy, instructive, and decisive experiences and events in one's life are those which are of daily occurrence; that the greatest riddle, displayed in full view of all, is seen by the fewest to be the greatest riddle, and that these problems are spread about in every direction, under the very feet of the passers-by, for the few real philosophers to lift up carefully, thenceforth to shine as diamonds of wisdom. Perhaps, in the short time now left us before the arrival of your friend, you will be good enough to tell us something of your experiences of university life, so as to close the circle of observations, to which we were involuntarily urged, respecting our educational institutions. We may also be allowed to remind you that you, at an earlier stage of your remarks, gave me the promise that you would do so. Starting with the public school, you claimed for it an extraordinary importance: all other institutions must be judged by its standard, according as its aim has been proposed; and, if its aim happens to be wrong, all the others have to suffer. Such an importance cannot now be adopted by the universities as a standard; for, by their present system of grouping, they would be nothing more than institutions where public school students might go through finishing courses. You promised me that you would explain this in greater detail later on: perhaps our student friends can bear witness to that, if they chanced to overhear that part of our conversation."

"We can testify to that," I put in. The philosopher then turned to us and said: "Well, if you really did listen attentively, perhaps you can now tell me what you understand by the expression 'the present aim of our public schools.' Besides, you are still near enough to this sphere to judge my opinions by the standard of your own impressions and experiences."

My friend instantly answered, quickly and smartly, as was his habit, in the following words: "Until now we had always thought that the sole object of the public school was to prepare students for the universities. This preparation, however, should tend to make us independent enough for the extraordinarily free position of a university student;[9] for it seems to me that a student, to a greater extent than any other individual, has more to decide and settle for himself. He must guide himself on a wide, utterly unknown

[9] The reader may be reminded that a German university student is subject to very few restrictions, and that much greater liberty is allowed him than is permitted to English students. Nietzsche did not approve of this extraordinary freedom, which, in his opinion, led to intellectual lawlessness.—Tr.

path for many years, so the public school must do its best to render him independent."

I continued the argument where my friend left off. "It even seems to me," I said, "that everything for which you have justly blamed the public school is only a necessary means employed to imbue the youthful student with some kind of independence, or at all events with the belief that there is such a thing. The teaching of German composition must be at the service of this independence: the individual must enjoy his opinions and carry out his designs early, so that he may be able to travel alone and without crutches. In this way he will soon be encouraged to produce original work, and still sooner to take up criticism and analysis. If Latin and Greek studies prove insufficient to make a student an enthusiastic admirer of antiquity, the methods with which such studies are pursued are at all events sufficient to awaken the scientific sense, the desire for a more strict causality of knowledge, the passion for finding out and inventing. Only think how many young men may be lured away for ever to the attractions of science by a new reading of some sort which they have snatched up with youthful hands at the public school! The public school boy must learn and collect a great deal of varied information: hence an impulse will gradually be created, accompanied with which he will continue to learn and collect independently at the university. We believe, in short, that the aim of the public school is to prepare and accustom the student always to live and learn independently afterwards, just as beforehand he must live and learn dependently at the public school."

The philosopher laughed, not altogether good-naturedly, and said: "You have just given me a fine example of that independence. And it is this very independence that shocks me so much, and makes any place in the neighbourhood of present-day students so disagreeable to me. Yes, my good friends, you are perfect, you are mature; nature has cast you and broken up the moulds, and your teachers must surely gloat over you. What liberty, certitude, and independence of judgment; what novelty and freshness of insight! You sit in judgment—and the cultures of all ages run away. The scientific sense is kindled, and rises out of you like a flame—let people be careful, lest you set them alight! If I go further into the question and look at your professors, I again find the same independence in a greater and even more charming degree: never was there a time so full of the most sublime independent folk, never was slavery more detested, the slavery of education and culture included.

"Permit me, however, to measure this independence of yours by the standard of this culture, and to consider your university as an educational institution and nothing else. If a foreigner desires to know something of the methods of our universities, he asks first of all with emphasis: 'How is the student connected with the university?' We answer: 'By the ear, as a hearer.' The foreigner is astonished. 'Only by the ear?' he repeats. 'Only by the ear,' we again reply. The student hears. When he speaks, when he sees, when he is in the company of his companions when he takes up some branch of art: in short, when he *lives*, he is independent, *i.e.* not dependent upon the educational institution. The student very often writes down something while he hears; and it is only at these rare moments that he hangs to the umbilical cord of his alma mater. He himself may choose what he is to listen to; he is not bound to believe what is said; he may close his ears if he does not care to hear. This is the 'acroamatic' method of teaching.

"The teacher, however, speaks to these listening students. Whatever else he may think and do is cut off from the student's perception by an immense gap. The professor often reads when he is speaking. As a rule he wishes to have as many hearers as possible; he is not content to have a few, and he is never satisfied with one only. One speaking mouth, with many ears, and half as many writing hands—there you have to all appearances, the external academical apparatus; the university engine of culture set in motion. Moreover, the proprietor of this one mouth is severed from and independent of the owners of the many ears; and this double independence is enthusiastically designated as 'academical freedom.' And again, that this freedom may be broadened still more, the one may speak what he likes and the other may hear what he likes; except that, behind both of them, at a modest distance, stands the State, with all the intentness of a supervisor, to remind the professors and students from time to time that *it* is the aim, the goal, the be-all and end-all, of this curious speaking and hearing procedure.

"We, who must be permitted to regard this phenomenon merely as an educational institution, will then inform the inquiring foreigner that what is called 'culture' in our universities merely proceeds from the mouth to the ear, and that every kind of training for culture is, as I said before, merely 'acroamatic.' Since, however, not only the hearing, but also the choice of what to hear is left to the independent decision of the liberal-minded and unprejudiced student, and since, again, he can withhold all belief and authority from what he hears, all training for culture, in the true sense of the term, reverts to himself; and the independence it was thought desirable to aim at in the public school now presents itself with the highest possible pride as 'academical self-training for culture,' and struts about in its brilliant plumage.

"Happy times, when youths are clever and cultured enough to teach themselves how to walk! Unsurpassable public schools, which succeed in implanting independence in the place of the dependence, discipline, subordination, and obedience implanted by former generations that thought it their duty to drive away all the bumptiousness of independence! Do you clearly see, my good friends, why I, from the standpoint of culture, regard the present type of university as a mere appendage to the public school? The culture instilled by the public school passes through the gates of the university as something ready and entire, and with its own particular claims: *it* demands, it gives laws, it sits in judgment. Do not, then, let yourselves be deceived in regard to the cultured student; for he, in so far as he thinks he has absorbed the blessings of education, is merely the public school boy as moulded by the hands of his teacher: one who, since his academical isolation, and after he has left the public school, has therefore been deprived of all further guidance to culture, that from now on he may begin to live by himself and be free.

"Free! Examine this freedom, ye observers of human nature! Erected upon the sandy, crumbling foundation of our present public school culture, its building slants to one side, trembling before the whirlwind's blast. Look at the free student, the herald of self-culture: guess what his instincts are; explain him from his needs! How does his culture appear to you when you measure it by three graduated scales: first, by his need for philosophy; second, by his instinct for art; and third, by Greek and Roman antiquity as the incarnate categorical imperative of all culture?

"Man is so much encompassed about by the most serious and difficult problems that, when they are brought to his attention in the right way, he is impelled betimes towards a lasting kind of philosophical wonder, from which alone, as a fruitful soil, a deep and noble culture can grow forth. His own experiences lead him most frequently to the consideration of these problems; and it is especially in the tempestuous period of youth that every personal event shines with a double gleam, both as the exemplification of a triviality and, at the same time, of an eternally surprising problem, deserving of explanation. At this age, which, as it were, sees his experiences encircled with metaphysical rainbows, man is, in the highest degree, in need of a guiding hand, because he has suddenly and almost instinctively convinced himself of the ambiguity of existence, and has lost the firm support of the beliefs he has hitherto held.

"This natural state of great need must of course be looked upon as the worst enemy of that beloved independence for which the cultured youth of the present day should be trained. All these sons of the present, who have raised the banner of the 'self-understood,' are therefore straining every nerve to crush down these feelings of youth, to cripple them, to mislead them, or to stop their growth altogether; and the favourite means employed is to paralyse that natural philosophic impulse by the so-called "historical culture." A still recent system,[10] which has won for itself a world-wide scandalous reputation, has discovered the formula for this self-destruction of philosophy; and now, wherever the historical view of things is found, we can see such a naive recklessness in bringing the irrational to 'rationality' and 'reason' and making black look like white, that one is even inclined to parody Hegel's phrase and ask: 'Is all this irrationality real?' Ah, it is only the irrational that now seems to be 'real,' *i.e.* really doing something; and to bring this kind of reality forward for the elucidation of history is reckoned as true 'historical culture.' It is into this that the philosophical impulse of our time has pupated itself; and the peculiar philosophers of our universities seem to have conspired to fortify and confirm the young academicians in it.

"It has thus come to pass that, in place of a profound interpretation of the eternally recurring problems, a historical—yea, even philological—balancing and questioning has entered into the educational arena: what this or that philosopher has or has not thought; whether this or that essay or dialogue is to be ascribed to him or not; or even whether this particular reading of a classical text is to be preferred to that. It is to neutral preoccupations with philosophy like these that our students in philosophical seminaries are stimulated; whence I have long accustomed myself to regard such science as a mere ramification of philology, and to value its representatives in proportion as they are good or bad philologists. So it has come about that *philosophy itself* is banished from the universities: wherewith our first question as to the value of our universities from the standpoint of culture is answered.

[10] Hegel's.—Tr.

"In what relationship these universities stand to *art* cannot be acknowledged without shame: in none at all. Of artistic thinking, learning, striving, and comparison, we do not find in them a single trace; and no one would seriously think that the voice of the universities would ever be raised to help the advancement of the higher national schemes of art. Whether an individual teacher feels himself to be personally qualified for art, or whether a professorial chair has been established for the training of æstheticising literary historians, does not enter into the question at all: the fact remains that the university is not in a position to control the young academician by severe artistic discipline, and that it must let happen what happens, willy-nilly—and this is the cutting answer to the immodest pretensions of the universities to represent themselves as the highest educational institutions.

"We find our academical 'independents' growing up without philosophy and without art; and how can they then have any need to 'go in for' the Greeks and Romans?—for we need now no longer pretend, like our forefathers, to have any great regard for Greece and Rome, which, besides, sit enthroned in almost inaccessible loneliness and majestic alienation. The universities of the present time consequently give no heed to almost extinct educational predilections like these, and found their philological chairs for the training of new and exclusive generations of philologists, who on their part give similar philological preparation in the public schools—a vicious circle which is useful neither to philologists nor to public schools, but which above all accuses the university for the third time of not being what it so pompously proclaims itself to be—a training ground for culture. Take away the Greeks, together with philosophy and art, and what ladder have you still remaining by which to ascend to culture? For, if you attempt to clamber up the ladder without these helps, you must permit me to inform you that all your learning will lie like a heavy burden on your shoulders rather than furnishing you with wings and bearing you aloft.

"If you honest thinkers have honourably remained in these three stages of intelligence, and have perceived that, in comparison with the Greeks, the modern student is unsuited to and unprepared for philosophy, that he has no truly artistic instincts, and is merely a barbarian believing himself to be free, you will not on this account turn away from him in disgust, although you will, of course, avoid coming into too close proximity with him. For, as he now is, *he is not to blame*: as you have perceived him he is the dumb but terrible accuser of those who are to blame.

“You should understand the secret language spoken by this guilty innocent, and then you, too, would learn to understand the inward state of that independence which is paraded outwardly with so much ostentation. Not one of these noble, well-qualified youths has remained a stranger to that restless, tiring, perplexing, and debilitating need of culture: during his university term, when he is apparently the only free man in a crowd of servants and officials, he atones for this huge illusion of freedom by ever-growing inner doubts and convictions. He feels that he can neither lead nor help himself; and then he plunges hopelessly into the workaday world and endeavours to ward off such feelings by study. The most trivial bustle fastens itself upon him; he sinks under his heavy burden. Then he suddenly pulls himself together; he still feels some of that power within him which would have enabled him to keep his head above water. Pride and noble resolutions assert themselves and grow in him. He is afraid of sinking at this early stage into the limits of a narrow profession; and now he grasps at pillars and railings alongside the stream that he may not be swept away by the current. In vain! for these supports give way, and he finds he has clutched at broken reeds. In low and despondent spirits he sees his plans vanish away in smoke. His condition is undignified, even dreadful: he keeps between the two extremes of work at high pressure and a state of melancholy enervation. Then he becomes tired, lazy, afraid of work, fearful of everything great; and hating himself. He looks into his own breast, analyses his faculties, and finds he is only peering into hollow and chaotic vacuity. And then he once more falls from the heights of his eagerly-desired self-knowledge into an ironical scepticism. He divests his struggles of their real importance, and feels himself ready to undertake any class of useful work, however degrading. He now seeks consolation in hasty and incessant action so as to hide himself from himself. And thus his helplessness and the want of a leader towards culture drive him from one form of life into another: but doubt, elevation, worry, hope, despair—everything flings him hither and thither as a proof that all the stars above him by which he could have guided his ship have set.

“There you have the picture of this glorious independence of yours, of that academical freedom, reflected in the highest minds—those which are truly in need of culture, compared with whom that other crowd of indifferent natures does not count at all, natures that delight in their freedom in a purely barbaric sense. For these latter show by their base smugness and their narrow professional limitations that this is the right element for them: against which there is nothing to be said. Their comfort, however, does not counterbalance the suffering of one single young man who has an inclination for culture and feels the need of a guiding hand, and who at last, in a moment of discontent, throws down the reins and begins to despise himself. This is the guiltless innocent; for who has saddled him with the unbearable burden of standing alone? Who has urged him on to independence at an age when one of the most natural and peremptory needs of youth is, so to speak, a self-surrendering to great leaders and an enthusiastic following in the footsteps of the masters?

"It is repulsive to consider the effects to which the violent suppression of such noble natures may lead. He who surveys the greatest supporters and friends of that pseudo-culture of the present time, which I so greatly detest, will only too frequently find among them such degenerate and shipwrecked men of culture, driven by inward despair to violent enmity against culture, when, in a moment of desperation, there was no one at hand to show them how to attain it. It is not the worst and most insignificant people whom we afterwards find acting as journalists and writers for the press in the metamorphosis of despair: the spirit of some well-known men of letters might even be described, and justly, as degenerate studentdom. How else, for example, can we reconcile that once well-known 'young Germany' with its present degenerate successors? Here we discover a need of culture which, so to speak, has grown mutinous, and which finally breaks out into the passionate cry: I am culture! There, before the gates of the public schools and universities, we can see the culture which has been driven like a fugitive away from these institutions. True, this culture is without the erudition of those establishments, but assumes nevertheless the mien of a sovereign; so that, for example, Gutzkow the novelist might be pointed to as the best example of a modern public school boy turned æsthete. Such a degenerate man of culture is a serious matter, and it is a horrifying spectacle for us to see that all our scholarly and journalistic publicity bears the stigma of this degeneracy upon it. How else can we do justice to our learned men, who pay untiring attention to, and even co-operate in the journalistic corruption of the people, how else than by the acknowledgment that their learning must fill a want of their own similar to that filled by novel-writing in the case of others: *i.e.* a flight from one's self, an ascetic extirpation of their cultural impulses, a desperate attempt to annihilate their own individuality. From our degenerate literary art, as also from that itch for scribbling of our learned men which has now reached such alarming proportions, wells forth the same sigh: Oh that we could forget ourselves! The attempt fails: memory, not yet suffocated by the mountains of printed paper under which it is buried, keeps on repeating from time to time: 'A degenerate man of culture! Born for culture and brought up to non-culture! Helpless barbarian, slave of the day, chained to the present moment, and thirsting for something—ever thirsting!'

"Oh, the miserable guilty innocents! For they lack something, a need that every one of them must have felt: a real educational institution, which could give them goals, masters, methods, companions; and from the midst of which the invigorating and uplifting breath of the true German spirit would inspire them. Thus they perish in the wilderness; thus they degenerate into enemies of that spirit which is at bottom closely allied to their own; thus they pile fault upon fault higher than any former generation ever did, soiling the clean, desecrating the holy, canonising the false and spurious. It is by them that you can judge the educational strength of our universities, asking yourselves, in all seriousness, the question: What cause did you promote through them? The German power of invention, the noble German desire for knowledge, the qualifying of the German for diligence and self-sacrifice—splendid and beautiful things, which other nations envy you; yea, the finest and most magnificent things in the world, if only that true German spirit overspread them like a dark thundercloud, pregnant with the blessing of forthcoming rain. But you are afraid of this spirit, and it has therefore come to pass that a cloud of another sort has thrown a heavy and oppressive atmosphere around your universities, in which your noble-minded scholars breathe wearily and with difficulty.

"A tragic, earnest, and instructive attempt was made in the present century to destroy the cloud I have last referred to, and also to turn the people's looks in the direction of the high welkin of the German spirit. In all the annals of our universities we cannot find any trace of a second attempt, and he who would impressively demonstrate what is now necessary for us will never find a better example. I refer to the old, primitive *Burschenschaft*.[11]

"When the war of liberation was over, the young student brought back home the unlooked-for and worthiest trophy of battle—the freedom of his fatherland. Crowned with this laurel he thought of something still nobler. On returning to the university, and finding that he was breathing heavily, he became conscious of that oppressive and contaminated air which overhung

[11] A German students' association, of liberal principles, founded for patriotic purposes at Jena in 1813.

the culture of the university. He suddenly saw, with horror-struck, wide-open eyes, the non-German barbarism, hiding itself in the guise of all kinds of scholasticism; he suddenly discovered that his own leaderless comrades were abandoned to a repulsive kind of youthful intoxication. And he was exasperated. He rose with the same aspect of proud indignation as Schiller may have had when reciting the *Robbers* to his companions: and if he had prefaced his drama with the picture of a lion, and the motto, 'in tyrannos,' his follower himself was that very lion preparing to spring; and every 'tyrant' began to tremble. Yes, if these indignant youths were looked at superficially and timorously, they would seem to be little else than Schiller's robbers: their talk sounded so wild to the anxious listener that Rome and Sparta seemed mere nunneries compared with these new spirits. The consternation raised by these young men was indeed far more general than had ever been caused by those other 'robbers' in court circles, of which a German prince, according to Goethe, is said to have expressed the opinion: 'If he had been God, and had foreseen the appearance of the *Robbers*, he would not have created the world.'

"Whence came the incomprehensible intensity of this alarm? For those young men were the bravest, purest, and most talented of the band both in dress and habits: they were distinguished by a magnanimous recklessness and a noble simplicity. A divine command bound them together to seek harder and more pious superiority: what could be feared from them? To what extent this fear was merely deceptive or simulated or really true is something that will probably never be exactly known; but a strong instinct spoke out of this fear and out of its disgraceful and senseless persecution. This instinct hated the Burschenschaft with an intense hatred for two reasons: first of all on account of its organisation, as being the first attempt to construct a true educational institution, and, secondly, on account of the spirit of this institution, that earnest, manly, stern, and daring German spirit; that spirit of the miner's son, Luther, which has come down to us unbroken from the time of the Reformation.

"Think of the *fate* of the Burschenschaft when I ask you, Did the German university then understand that spirit, as even the German princes in their hatred appear to have understood it? Did the alma mater boldly and resolutely throw her protecting arms round her noble sons and say: 'You must kill me first, before you touch my children?' I hear your answer—by it you may judge whether the German university is an educational institution or not.

"The student knew at that time at what depth a true educational institution must take root, namely, in an inward renovation and inspiration of the purest moral faculties. And this must always be repeated to the student's credit. He may have learnt on the field of battle what he could learn least of all in the sphere of 'academical freedom': that great leaders are necessary, and that all culture begins with obedience. And in the midst of victory, with his thoughts turned to his liberated fatherland, he made the vow that he would remain German. German! Now he learnt to understand his Tacitus; now he grasped the signification of Kant's categorical imperative; now he was enraptured by Weber's "Lyre and Sword" songs.[12] The gates of philosophy, of art, yea, even of antiquity, opened unto him; and in one of the most memorable of bloody acts, the murder of Kotzebue, he revenged—with penetrating insight and enthusiastic short-sightedness—his one and only Schiller, prematurely consumed by the opposition of the stupid world: Schiller, who could have been his leader, master, and organiser, and whose loss he now bewailed with such heartfelt resentment.

"For that was the doom of those promising students: they did not find the leaders they wanted. They gradually became uncertain, discontented, and at variance among themselves; unlucky indiscretions showed only too soon that the one indispensability of powerful minds was lacking in the midst of them: and, while that mysterious murder gave evidence of astonishing strength, it gave no less evidence of the grave danger arising from the want of a leader. They were leaderless—therefore they perished.

"For I repeat it, my friends! All culture begins with the very opposite of that which is now so highly esteemed as 'academical freedom': with obedience, with subordination, with discipline, with subjection. And as leaders must have followers so also must the followers have a leader—here a certain reciprocal predisposition prevails in the hierarchy of spirits: yea,

[12] Weber set one or two of Körner's "Lyre and Sword" songs to music. The reader will remember that these lectures were delivered when Nietzsche was only in his twenty-eighth year. Like Goethe, he afterwards freed himself from all patriotic trammels and prejudices, and aimed at a general European culture. Luther, Schiller, Kant, Körner, and Weber did not continue to be the objects of his veneration for long, indeed, they were afterwards violently attacked by him, and the superficial student who speaks of inconsistency may be reminded of Nietzsche's phrase in stanza 12 of the epilogue to *Beyond Good and Evil*: "Nur wer sich wandelt, bleibt mit mir verwandt"; *i.e.* only the changing ones have anything in common with me.—TR.

a kind of pre-established harmony. This eternal hierarchy, towards which all things naturally tend, is always threatened by that pseudo-culture which now sits on the throne of the present. It endeavours either to bring the leaders down to the level of its own servitude or else to cast them out altogether. It seduces the followers when they are seeking their predestined leader, and overcomes them by the fumes of its narcotics. When, however, in spite of all this, leader and followers have at last met, wounded and sore, there is an impassioned feeling of rapture, like the echo of an ever-sounding lyre, a feeling which I can let you divine only by means of a simile.

"Have you ever, at a musical rehearsal, looked at the strange, shrivelled-up, good-natured species of men who usually form the German orchestra? What changes and fluctuations we see in that capricious goddess 'form'! What noses and ears, what clumsy, *danse macabre* movements! Just imagine for a moment that you were deaf, and had never dreamed of the existence of sound or music, and that you were looking upon the orchestra as a company of actors, and trying to enjoy their performance as a drama and nothing more. Undisturbed by the idealising effect of the sound, you could never see enough of the stern, medieval, wood-cutting movement of this comical spectacle, this harmonious parody on the *homo sapiens*.

"Now, on the other hand, assume that your musical sense has returned, and that your ears are opened. Look at the honest conductor at the head of the orchestra performing his duties in a dull, spiritless fashion: you no longer think of the comical aspect of the whole scene, you listen—but it seems to you that the spirit of tediousness spreads out from the honest conductor over all his companions. Now you see only torpidity and flabbiness, you hear only the trivial, the rhythmically inaccurate, and the melodiously trite. You see the orchestra only as an indifferent, ill-humoured, and even wearisome crowd of players.

"But set a genius—a real genius—in the midst of this crowd; and you instantly perceive something almost incredible. It is as if this genius, in his lightning transmigration, had entered into these mechanical, lifeless bodies, and as if only one demoniacal eye gleamed forth out of them all. Now look and listen—you can never listen enough! When you again observe the orchestra, now loftily storming, now fervently wailing, when you notice the quick tightening of every muscle and the rhythmical necessity of every gesture, then you too will feel what a pre-established harmony there is between leader and followers, and how in the hierarchy of spirits everything impels us towards the establishment of a like organisation. You can divine from my simile what I would understand by a true educational institution, and why I am very far from recognising one in the present type of university."

> [From a few MS. notes written down by Nietzsche in the spring and autumn of 1872, and still preserved in the Nietzsche Archives at Weimar, it is evident that he at one time intended to add a sixth and seventh lecture to the five just given. These notes, although included in the latest edition of Nietzsche's works, are utterly lacking in interest and continuity, being merely headings and sub-headings of sections in the proposed lectures. They do not, indeed, occupy more than two printed pages, and were deemed too fragmentary for translation in this edition.]

HOMER
AND CLASSICAL PHILOLOGY

(Inaugural Address delivered at Bâle University, 28th of May 1869.)

Homer and Classical Philology.

AT the present day no clear and consistent opinion seems to be held regarding Classical Philology. We are conscious of this in the circles of the learned just as much as among the followers of that science itself. The cause of this lies in its many-sided character, in the lack of an abstract unity, and in the inorganic aggregation of heterogeneous scientific activities which are connected with one another only by the name "Philology." It must be freely admitted that philology is to some extent borrowed from several other sciences, and is mixed together like a magic potion from the most outlandish liquors, ores, and bones. It may even be added that it likewise conceals within itself an artistic element, one which, on æsthetic and ethical grounds, may be called imperatival—an element that acts in opposition to its purely scientific behaviour. Philology is composed of history just as much as of natural science or æsthetics: history, in so far as it endeavours to comprehend the manifestations of the individualities of peoples in ever new images, and the prevailing law in the disappearance of phenomena; natural science, in so far as it strives to fathom the deepest instinct of man, that of speech; æsthetics, finally, because from various antiquities at our disposal it endeavours to pick out the so-called "classical" antiquity, with the view and pretension of excavating the ideal world buried under it, and to hold up to the present the mirror of the classical and everlasting standards. That these wholly different scientific and æsthetico-ethical impulses have been associated under a common name, a kind of sham monarchy, is shown especially by the fact that philology at every period from its origin onwards was at the same time pedagogical. From the standpoint of the pedagogue, a choice was offered of those elements which were of the greatest educational value; and thus that science, or at least that scientific aim, which we call philology, gradually developed out of the practical calling originated by the exigencies of that science itself.

These philological aims were pursued sometimes with greater ardour and sometimes with less, in accordance with the degree of culture and the development of the taste of a particular period; but, on the other hand, the followers of this science are in the habit of regarding the aims which correspond to their several abilities as *the* aims of philology; whence it comes about that the estimation of philology in public opinion depends upon the weight of the personalities of the philologists!

At the present time—that is to say, in a period which has seen men distinguished in almost every department of philology—a general uncertainty of judgment has increased more and more, and likewise a general relaxation of interest and participation in philological problems. Such an undecided and imperfect state of public opinion is damaging to a science in that its hidden and open enemies can work with much better prospects of success. And philology has a great many such enemies. Where do we not meet with them, these mockers, always ready to aim a blow at the philological "moles," the animals that practise dust-eating *ex professo*, and that grub up and eat for the eleventh time what they have already eaten ten times before. For opponents of this sort, however, philology is merely a useless, harmless, and inoffensive pastime, an object of laughter and not of hate. But, on the other hand, there is a boundless and infuriated hatred of philology wherever an ideal, as such, is feared, where the modern man falls down to worship himself, and where Hellenism is looked upon as a superseded and hence very insignificant point of view. Against these enemies, we philologists must always count upon the assistance of artists and men of artistic minds; for they alone can judge how the sword of barbarism sweeps over the head of every one who loses sight of the unutterable simplicity and noble dignity of the Hellene; and how no progress in commerce or technical industries, however brilliant, no school regulations, no political education of the masses, however widespread and complete, can protect us from the curse of ridiculous and barbaric offences against good taste, or from annihilation by the Gorgon head of the classicist.

Whilst philology as a whole is looked on with jealous eyes by these two classes of opponents, there are numerous and varied hostilities in other directions of philology; philologists themselves are quarrelling with one another; internal dissensions are caused by useless disputes about precedence and mutual jealousies, but especially by the differences—even enmities—comprised in the name of philology, which are not, however, by any means naturally harmonised instincts.

Science has this in common with art, that the most ordinary, everyday thing appears to it as something entirely new and attractive, as if metamorphosed by witchcraft and now seen for the first time. Life is worth living, says art, the beautiful temptress; life is worth knowing, says science. With this contrast the so heartrending and dogmatic tradition follows in a *theory*, and consequently in the practice of classical philology derived from this theory. We may consider antiquity from a scientific point of view; we may try to look at what has happened with the eye of a historian, or to arrange and compare the linguistic forms of ancient masterpieces, to bring them at all events under a morphological law; but we always lose the wonderful creative force, the real fragrance, of the atmosphere of antiquity; we forget that passionate emotion which instinctively drove our meditation and enjoyment back to the Greeks. From this point onwards we must take notice of a clearly determined and very surprising antagonism which philology has great cause to regret. From the circles upon whose help we must place the most implicit reliance—the artistic friends of antiquity, the warm supporters of Hellenic beauty and noble simplicity—we hear harsh voices crying out that it is precisely the philologists themselves who are the real opponents and destroyers of the ideals of antiquity. Schiller upbraided the philologists with having scattered Homer's laurel crown to the winds. It was none other than Goethe who, in early life a supporter of Wolf's theories regarding Homer, recanted in the verses—

With subtle wit you took away
Our former adoration:
The Iliad, you may us say,
Was mere conglomeration.
Think it not crime in any way:
Youth's fervent adoration
Leads us to know the verity,
And feel the poet's unity.

The reason of this want of piety and reverence must lie deeper; and many are in doubt as to whether philologists are lacking in artistic capacity and impressions, so that they are unable to do justice to the ideal, or whether the spirit of negation has become a destructive and iconoclastic principle of theirs. When, however, even the friends of antiquity, possessed of such doubts and hesitations, point to our present classical philology as something questionable, what influence may we not ascribe to the outbursts of the "realists" and the claptrap of the heroes of the passing hour? To answer the latter on this occasion, especially when we consider the nature of the present assembly, would be highly injudicious; at any rate, if I do not wish to meet with the fate of that sophist who, when in Sparta, publicly undertook to praise and defend Herakles, when he was interrupted with the query: "But who then has found fault with him?" I cannot help thinking, however, that some of these scruples are still sounding in the ears of not a few in this gathering; for they may still be frequently heard from the lips of noble and artistically gifted men—as even an upright philologist must feel them, and feel them most painfully, at moments when his spirits are downcast. For the single individual there is no deliverance from the dissensions referred to; but what we contend and inscribe on our banner is the fact that classical philology, as a whole, has nothing whatsoever to do with the quarrels and bickerings of its individual disciples. The entire scientific and artistic movement of this peculiar centaur is bent, though with cyclopic slowness, upon bridging over the gulf between the ideal antiquity—which is perhaps only the magnificent blossoming of the Teutonic longing for the south—and the real antiquity; and thus classical philology pursues only the final end of its own being, which is the fusing together of primarily hostile impulses that have only forcibly been brought together. Let us talk as we will about the unattainability of this goal, and even designate the goal itself as an illogical pretension—the aspiration for it is very real; and I should like to try to make it clear by an example that the most significant steps of classical philology never lead away from the ideal antiquity, but to it; and that, just when people are speaking unwarrantably of the overthrow of sacred shrines, new and more worthy altars are being erected. Let us then examine the so-called *Homeric question* from this standpoint, a question the most important problem of which Schiller called a scholastic barbarism.

The important problem referred to is *the question of the personality of Homer*.

We now meet everywhere with the firm opinion that the question of Homer's personality is no longer timely, and that it is quite a different thing from the real "Homeric question." It may be added that, for a given period—such as our present philological period, for example—the centre of discussion may be removed from the problem of the poet's personality; for even now a painstaking experiment is being made to reconstruct the

Homeric poems without the aid of personality, treating them as the work of several different persons. But if the centre of a scientific question is rightly seen to be where the swelling tide of new views has risen up, *i.e.* where individual scientific investigation comes into contact with the whole life of science and culture—if any one, in other words, indicates a historico-cultural valuation as the central point of the question, he must also, in the province of Homeric criticism, take his stand upon the question of personality as being the really fruitful oasis in the desert of the whole argument. For in Homer the modern world, I will not say has learnt, but has examined, a great historical point of view; and, even without now putting forward my own opinion as to whether this examination has been or can be happily carried out, it was at all events the first example of the application of that productive point of view. By it scholars learnt to recognise condensed beliefs in the apparently firm, immobile figures of the life of ancient peoples; by it they for the first time perceived the wonderful capability of the soul of a people to represent the conditions of its morals and beliefs in the form of a personality. When historical criticism has confidently seized upon this method of evaporating apparently concrete personalities, it is permissible to point to the first experiment as an important event in the history of sciences, without considering whether it was successful in this instance or not.

It is a common occurrence for a series of striking signs and wonderful emotions to precede an epoch-making discovery. Even the experiment I have just referred to has its own attractive history; but it goes back to a surprisingly ancient era. Friedrich August Wolf has exactly indicated the spot where Greek antiquity dropped the question. The zenith of the historico-literary studies of the Greeks, and hence also of their point of greatest importance—the Homeric question—was reached in the age of the Alexandrian grammarians. Up to this time the Homeric question had run through the long chain of a uniform process of development, of which the standpoint of those grammarians seemed to be the last link, the last, indeed, which was attainable by antiquity. They conceived the *Iliad* and the *Odyssey* as the creations of *one single* Homer; they declared it to be psychologically possible for two such different works to have sprung from the brain of *one* genius, in contradiction to the Chorizontes, who represented the extreme limit of the scepticism of a few detached individuals of antiquity rather than antiquity itself considered as a whole. To explain the different general impression of the two books on the assumption that *one* poet composed them both, scholars sought assistance by referring to the seasons of the poet's life, and compared the poet of the *Odyssey* to the setting sun. The eyes of those critics were tirelessly on the lookout for discrepancies in the language and thoughts of the two poems; but at this time also a history of the Homeric poem and its tradition was prepared, according to which these discrepancies were not due to Homer, but to those who committed his words to writing and those who sang them. It was believed that Homer's poem was passed from one generation to another *viva voce*, and faults were attributed to the improvising and at times forgetful bards. At a certain given date, about the time of Pisistratus, the poems which had been repeated orally were said to have been collected in manuscript form; but the scribes, it is added, allowed themselves to take some liberties with the text by transposing some lines and adding extraneous matter here and there. This entire hypothesis is the most important in the domain of literary studies that antiquity has exhibited; and the acknowledgment of the dissemination of the Homeric poems by word of mouth, as opposed to the habits of a book-learned age, shows in particular a depth of ancient sagacity worthy of our admiration. From those times until the generation that produced Friedrich August Wolf we must take a jump over a long historical vacuum; but in our own age we find the argument left just as it was at the time when the power of controversy departed from antiquity, and it is a matter of indifference to us that Wolf accepted as certain tradition what antiquity itself had set up only as a hypothesis. It may be remarked as most characteristic of this hypothesis that, in the strictest sense, the personality of Homer is treated seriously; that a certain standard of inner harmony is everywhere presupposed in the manifestations of the personality; and that, with these two excellent auxiliary hypotheses, whatever is seen to be below this standard and opposed to this inner harmony is at once swept aside as un-Homeric. But even this distinguishing characteristic, in place of wishing to recognise the supernatural existence of a tangible personality, ascends likewise through all the stages that lead to that zenith, with ever-increasing energy and clearness. Individuality is ever more strongly felt and accentuated; the psychological possibility of a *single* Homer is ever more forcibly demanded. If we descend backwards from this zenith, step by step, we find a guide to the understanding of the Homeric problem in the person of Aristotle. Homer was for him the flawless and untiring artist who knew his end and the means to attain it; but there is still a trace of infantile criticism to be found in Aristotle—*i.e.*, in the naive concession he made to the public opinion that considered Homer as the author of the original of all comic epics, the *Margites*. If we go still further backwards from Aristotle, the inability to create a personality is seen to increase; more and more poems are attributed to Homer; and every period lets us see its degree of criticism by how much and what it considers as Homeric. In this backward examination, we instinctively feel that away beyond Herodotus there lies a period in which an immense flood of great epics has been identified with the name of Homer.

Let us imagine ourselves as living in the time of Pisistratus: the word "Homer" then comprehended an abundance of dissimilarities. What was meant by "Homer" at that time? It is evident that that generation found itself unable to grasp a personality and the limits of its manifestations. Homer had now become of small consequence. And then we meet with the weighty question: What lies before this period? Has Homer's personality, because it cannot be grasped, gradually faded away into an empty name? Or had all the Homeric poems been gathered together in a body, the nation naively representing itself by the figure of Homer? *Was the person created out of a conception, or the conception out of a person?* This is the real "Homeric question," the central problem of the personality.

The difficulty of answering this question, however, is increased when we seek a reply in another direction, from the standpoint of the poems themselves which have come down to us. As it is difficult for us at the present day, and necessitates a serious effort on our part, to understand the law of gravitation clearly—that the earth alters its form of motion when another heavenly body changes its position in space, although no material connection unites one to the other—it likewise costs us some trouble to obtain a clear impression of that wonderful problem which, like a coin long passed from hand to hand, has lost its original and highly conspicuous stamp. Poetical works, which cause the hearts of even the greatest geniuses to fail when they endeavour to vie with them, and in which unsurpassable images are held up for the admiration of posterity—and yet the poet who wrote them with only a hollow, shaky name, whenever we do lay hold on him; nowhere the solid kernel of a powerful personality. "For who would wage war with the gods: who, even with the one god?" asks Goethe even, who, though a genius, strove in vain to solve that mysterious problem of the Homeric inaccessibility.

The conception of popular poetry seemed to lead like a bridge over this problem—a deeper and more original power than that of every single creative individual was said to have become active; the happiest people, in the happiest period of its existence, in the highest activity of fantasy and formative power, was said to have created those immeasurable poems. In this universality there is something almost intoxicating in the thought of a popular poem: we feel, with artistic pleasure, the broad, overpowering liberation of a popular gift, and we delight in this natural phenomenon as we do in an uncontrollable cataract. But as soon as we examine this thought at close quarters, we involuntarily put a poetic *mass of people* in the place of the poetising *soul of the people*: a long row of popular poets in whom individuality has no meaning, and in whom the tumultuous movement of a people's soul, the intuitive strength of a people's eye, and the unabated profusion of a people's fantasy, were once powerful: a row of original geniuses, attached to a time, to a poetic genus, to a subject-matter.

Such a conception justly made people suspicious. Could it be possible that that same Nature who so sparingly distributed her rarest and most precious production—genius—should suddenly take the notion of lavishing her gifts in one sole direction? And here the thorny question again made its appearance: Could we not get along with one genius only, and explain the present existence of that unattainable excellence? And now eyes were keenly on the lookout for whatever that excellence and singularity might consist of. Impossible for it to be in the construction of the complete works, said one party, for this is far from faultless; but doubtless to be found in single songs: in the single pieces above all; not in the whole. A second party, on the other hand, sheltered themselves beneath the authority of Aristotle, who especially admired Homer's "divine" nature in the choice of his entire subject, and the manner in which he planned and carried it out. If, however, this construction was not clearly seen, this fault was due to the way the poems were handed down to posterity and not to the poet himself—it was the result of retouchings and interpolations, owing to which the original setting of the work gradually became obscured. The more the first school looked for inequalities, contradictions, perplexities, the more energetically did the other school brush aside what in their opinion obscured the original plan, in order, if possible, that nothing might be left remaining but the actual words of the original epic itself. The second school of thought of course held fast by the conception of an epoch-making genius as the composer of the great works. The first school, on the other hand, wavered between the supposition of one genius plus a number of minor poets, and another hypothesis which assumed only a number of superior and even mediocre individual bards, but also postulated a mysterious discharging, a deep, national, artistic impulse, which shows itself in individual minstrels as an almost indifferent medium. It is to this latter school that we must attribute the representation of the Homeric poems as the expression of that mysterious impulse.

All these schools of thought start from the assumption that the problem of the present form of these epics can be solved from the standpoint of an æsthetic judgment—but we must await the decision as to the authorised line of demarcation between the man of genius and the poetical soul of the people. Are there characteristic differences between the utterances of the *man of genius* and the *poetical soul of the people*?

This whole contrast, however, is unjust and misleading. There is no more dangerous assumption in modern æsthetics than that of *popular poetry* and *individual poetry*, or, as it is usually called, *artistic poetry*. This is the reaction, or, if you will, the superstition, which followed upon the most momentous discovery of historico-philological science, the discovery and appreciation of the *soul of the people*. For this discovery prepared the way for a coming scientific view of history, which was until then, and in many respects is even now, a mere collection of materials, with the prospect that new materials would continue to be added, and that the huge, overflowing pile would never be systematically arranged. The people now understood for the first time that the long-felt power of greater individualities and wills was larger than the pitifully small will of an individual man;[13] they now saw that everything truly great in the kingdom of the will could not have its deepest root in the inefficacious and ephemeral individual will; and, finally, they now discovered the powerful instincts of the masses, and diagnosed those unconscious impulses to be the foundations and supports of the so-called universal history. But the newly-lighted flame also cast its shadow: and this shadow was none other than that superstition already referred to, which popular poetry set up in opposition to individual poetry, and thus enlarged the comprehension of the people's soul to that of the people's mind. By the misapplication of a tempting analogical inference, people had reached the point of applying in the domain of the intellect and artistic ideas that principle of greater individuality which is truly applicable only in the domain of the will. The masses have never experienced more flattering treatment than in thus having the laurel of genius set upon their empty heads. It was imagined that new shells were forming round a small kernel, so to speak, and that those pieces of popular poetry originated like

[13] Of course Nietzsche saw afterwards that this was not so.—Tr.

avalanches, in the drift and flow of tradition. They were, however, ready to consider that kernel as being of the smallest possible dimensions, so that they might occasionally get rid of it altogether without losing anything of the mass of the avalanche. According to this view, the text itself and the stories built round it are one and the same thing.

Now, however, such a contrast between popular poetry and individual poetry does not exist at all; on the contrary, all poetry, and of course popular poetry also, requires an intermediary individuality. This much-abused contrast, therefore, is necessary only when the term *individual poem* is understood to mean a poem which has not grown out of the soil of popular feeling, but which has been composed by a non-popular poet in a non-popular atmosphere—something which has come to maturity in the study of a learned man, for example.

With the superstition which presupposes poetising masses is connected another: that popular poetry is limited to one particular period of a people's history and afterwards dies out—which indeed follows as a consequence of the first superstition I have mentioned. According to this school, in the place of the gradually decaying popular poetry we have artistic poetry, the work of individual minds, not of masses of people. But the same powers which were once active are still so; and the form in which they act has remained exactly the same. The great poet of a literary period is still a popular poet in no narrower sense than the popular poet of an illiterate age. The difference between them is not in the way they originate, but it is their diffusion and propagation, in short, *tradition*. This tradition is exposed to eternal danger without the help of handwriting, and runs the risk of including in the poems the remains of those individualities through whose oral tradition they were handed down.

If we apply all these principles to the Homeric poems, it follows that we gain nothing with our theory of the poetising soul of the people, and that we are always referred back to the poetical individual. We are thus confronted with the task of distinguishing that which can have originated only in a single poetical mind from that which is, so to speak, swept up by the tide of oral tradition, and which is a highly important constituent part of the Homeric poems.

Since literary history first ceased to be a mere collection of names, people have attempted to grasp and formulate the individualities of the poets. A certain mechanism forms part of the method: it must be explained—*i.e.*, it must be deduced from principles—why this or that individuality appears in this way and not in that. People now study biographical details, environment, acquaintances, contemporary events, and believe that by mixing all these ingredients together they will be able to manufacture the wished-for individuality. But they forget that the *punctum saliens*, the indefinable individual characteristics, can never be obtained from a compound of this nature. The less there is known about the life and times of the poet, the less applicable is this mechanism. When, however, we have merely the works and the name of the writer, it is almost impossible to detect the individuality, at all events, for those who put their faith in the mechanism in question; and particularly when the works are perfect, when they are pieces of popular poetry. For the best way for these mechanicians to grasp individual characteristics is by perceiving deviations from the genius of the people; the aberrations and hidden allusions: and the fewer discrepancies to be found in a poem the fainter will be the traces of the individual poet who composed it.

All those deviations, everything dull and below the ordinary standard which scholars think they perceive in the Homeric poems, were attributed to tradition, which thus became the scapegoat. What was left of Homer's own individual work? Nothing but a series of beautiful and prominent passages chosen in accordance with subjective taste. The sum total of æsthetic singularity which every individual scholar perceived with his own artistic gifts, he now called Homer.

This is the central point of the Homeric errors. The name of Homer, from the very beginning, has no connection either with the conception of æsthetic perfection or yet with the *Iliad* and the *Odyssey*. Homer as the composer of the *Iliad* and the *Odyssey* is not a historical tradition, but an *æsthetic judgment*.

The only path which leads back beyond the time of Pisistratus and helps us to elucidate the meaning of the name Homer, takes its way on the one hand through the reports which have reached us concerning Homer's birthplace: from which we see that, although his name is always associated with heroic epic poems, he is on the other hand no more referred to as the composer of the *Iliad* and the *Odyssey* than as the author of the *Thebais* or any other cyclical epic. On the other hand, again, an old tradition tells of the contest between Homer and Hesiod, which proves that when these two names were mentioned people instinctively thought of two epic tendencies, the heroic and the didactic; and that the signification of the name "Homer" was included in the material category and not in the formal. This imaginary contest with Hesiod did not even yet show the faintest presentiment of individuality. From the time of Pisistratus onwards, however, with the surprisingly rapid development of the Greek feeling for beauty, the differences in the æsthetic value of those epics continued to be felt more and more: the *Iliad* and the *Odyssey* arose from the depths of the flood and have remained on the surface ever since. With this process of æsthetic separation, the conception of Homer gradually became narrower: the old material meaning of the name "Homer" as the father of the heroic epic poem, was changed into the æsthetic meaning of Homer, the father of poetry in general, and likewise its original prototype. This transformation was contemporary with the rationalistic criticism which made Homer the magician out to be a possible poet, which vindicated the material and formal traditions of those numerous epics as against the unity of the poet, and gradually removed that heavy load of cyclical epics from Homer's shoulders.

So Homer, the poet of the *Iliad* and the *Odyssey*, is an æsthetic judgment. It is, however, by no means affirmed against the poet of these epics that he was merely the imaginary being of an æsthetic impossibility, which can be the opinion of only very few philologists indeed. The majority contend that a single individual was responsible for the general design of a poem such as the *Iliad*, and further that this individual was Homer. The first part of this contention may be admitted; but, in accordance with what I have said, the latter part must be denied. And I very much doubt whether the majority of those who adopt the first part of the contention have taken the following considerations into account.

The design of an epic such as the *Iliad* is not an entire *whole*, not an organism; but a number of pieces strung together, a collection of reflections arranged in accordance with æsthetic rules. It is certainly the standard of an artist's greatness to note what he can take in with a single glance and set out in rhythmical form. The infinite profusion of images and incidents in the Homeric epic must force us to admit that such a wide range of vision is next to impossible. Where, however, a poet is unable to observe artistically with a single glance, he usually piles conception on conception, and endeavours to adjust his characters according to a comprehensive scheme.

He will succeed in this all the better the more he is familiar with the fundamental principles of æsthetics: he will even make some believe that he made himself master of the entire subject by a single powerful glance.

The *Iliad* is not a garland, but a bunch of flowers. As many pictures as possible are crowded on one canvas; but the man who placed them there was indifferent as to whether the grouping of the collected pictures was invariably suitable and rhythmically beautiful. He well knew that no one would ever consider the collection as a whole; but would merely look at the individual parts. But that stringing together of some pieces as the manifestations of a grasp of art which was not yet highly developed, still less thoroughly comprehended and generally esteemed, cannot have been the real Homeric deed, the real Homeric epoch-making event. On the contrary, this design is a later product, far later than Homer's celebrity. Those, therefore, who look for the "original and perfect design" are looking for a mere phantom; for the dangerous path of oral tradition had reached its end just as the systematic arrangement appeared on the scene; the disfigurements which were caused on the way could not have affected the design, for this did not form part of the material handed down from generation to generation.

The relative imperfection of the design must not, however, prevent us from seeing in the designer a different personality from the real poet. It is not only probable that everything which was created in those times with conscious æsthetic insight, was infinitely inferior to the songs that sprang up naturally in the poet's mind and were written down with instinctive power: we can even take a step further. If we include the so-called cyclic poems in this comparison, there remains for the designer of the *Iliad* and the *Odyssey* the indisputable merit of having done something relatively great in this conscious technical composing: a merit which we might have been prepared to recognise from the beginning, and which is in my opinion of the very first order in the domain of instinctive creation. We may even be ready to pronounce this synthetisation of great importance. All those dull passages and discrepancies—deemed of such importance, but really only subjective, which we usually look upon as the petrified remains of the period of tradition—are not these perhaps merely the almost necessary evils which must fall to the lot of the poet of genius who undertakes a composition virtually without a parallel, and, further, one which proves to be of incalculable difficulty?

Let it be noted that the insight into the most diverse operations of the instinctive and the conscious changes the position of the Homeric problem; and in my opinion throws light upon it.

We believe in a great poet as the author of the *Iliad* and the *Odyssey*—*but not that Homer was this poet*.

The decision on this point has already been given. The generation that invented those numerous Homeric fables, that poetised the myth of the contest between Homer and Hesiod, and looked upon all the poems of the epic cycle as Homeric, did not feel an æsthetic but a material singularity when it pronounced the name "Homer." This period regards Homer as belonging to the ranks of artists like Orpheus, Eumolpus, Dædalus, and Olympus, the mythical discoverers of a new branch of art, to whom, therefore, all the later fruits which grew from the new branch were thankfully dedicated.

And that wonderful genius to whom we owe the *Iliad* and the *Odyssey* belongs to this thankful posterity: he, too, sacrificed his name on the altar of the primeval father of the Homeric epic, Homeros.

Up to this point, gentlemen, I think I have been able to put before you the fundamental philosophical and æsthetic characteristics of the problem of the personality of Homer, keeping all minor details rigorously at a distance, on the supposition that the primary form of this widespread and honeycombed mountain known as the Homeric question can be most clearly observed by looking down at it from a far-off height. But I have also, I imagine, recalled two facts to those friends of antiquity who take such delight in accusing us philologists of lack of piety for great conceptions and an unproductive zeal for destruction. In the first place, those "great" conceptions—such, for example, as that of the indivisible and inviolable poetic genius, Homer—were during the pre-Wolfian period only too great, and hence inwardly altogether empty and elusive when we now try to grasp them. If classical philology goes back again to the same conceptions, and once more tries to pour new wine into old bottles, it is only on the surface that the conceptions are the same: everything has really become new; bottle and mind, wine and word. We everywhere find traces of the fact that philology has lived in company with poets, thinkers, and artists for the last hundred years: whence it has now come about that the heap of ashes formerly pointed to as classical philology is now turned into fruitful and even rich soil.[14]

And there is a second fact which I should like to recall to the memory of those friends of antiquity who turn their dissatisfied backs on classical philology. You honour the immortal masterpieces of the Hellenic mind in

[14] Nietzsche perceived later on that this statement was, unfortunately, not justified.—Tr.

poetry and sculpture, and think yourselves so much more fortunate than preceding generations, which had to do without them; but you must not forget that this whole fairyland once lay buried under mountains of prejudice, and that the blood and sweat and arduous labour of innumerable followers of our science were all necessary to lift up that world from the chasm into which it had sunk. We grant that philology is not the creator of this world, not the composer of that immortal music; but is it not a merit, and a great merit, to be a mere virtuoso, and let the world for the first time hear that music which lay so long in obscurity, despised and undecipherable? Who was Homer previously to Wolf's brilliant investigations? A good old man, known at best as a "natural genius," at all events the child of a barbaric age, replete with faults against good taste and good morals. Let us hear how a learned man of the first rank writes about Homer even so late as 1783: "Where does the good man live? Why did he remain so long incognito? Apropos, can't you get me a silhouette of him?"

We demand *thanks*—not in our own name, for we are but atoms—but in the name of philology itself, which is indeed neither a Muse nor a Grace, but a messenger of the gods: and just as the Muses descended upon the dull and tormented Boeotian peasants, so Philology comes into a world full of gloomy colours and pictures, full of the deepest, most incurable woes; and speaks to men comfortingly of the beautiful and godlike figure of a distant, rosy, and happy fairyland.

It is time to close; yet before I do so a few words of a personal character must be added, justified, I hope, by the occasion of this lecture.

It is but right that a philologist should describe his end and the means to it in the short formula of a confession of faith; and let this be done in the saying of Seneca which I thus reverse—

"Philosophia facta est quæ philologia fuit."

By this I wish to signify that all philological activities should be enclosed and surrounded by a philosophical view of things, in which everything individual and isolated is evaporated as something detestable, and in which great homogeneous views alone remain. Now, therefore, that I have enunciated my philological creed, I trust you will give me cause to hope that I shall no longer be a stranger among you: give me the assurance that in working with you towards this end I am worthily fulfilling the confidence with which the highest authorities of this community have honoured me.

Printed by Libri Plureos GmbH in Hamburg,
Germany